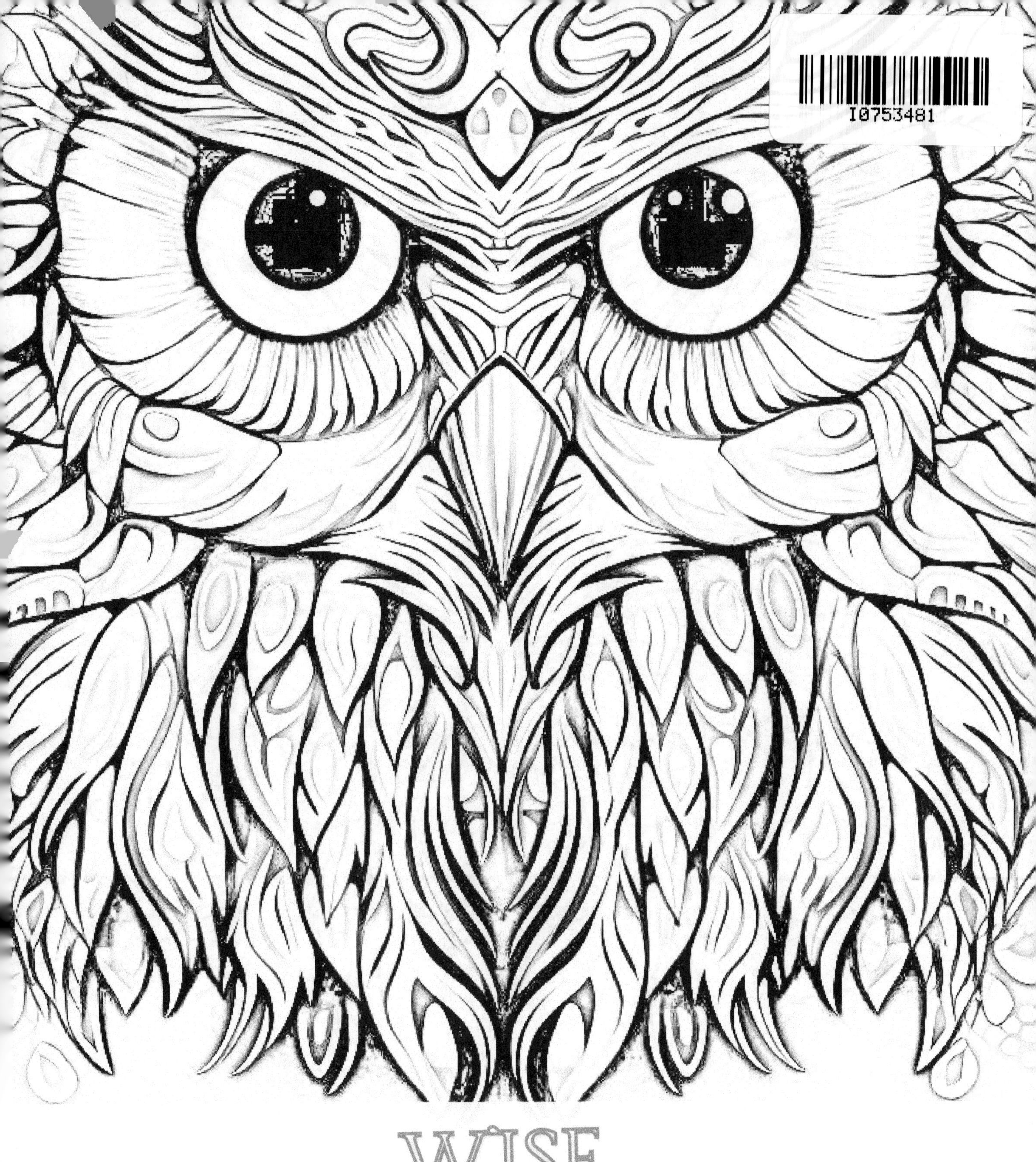

WISE

I am insightful, trusting my instincts and knowledge to guide me through life's challenges.

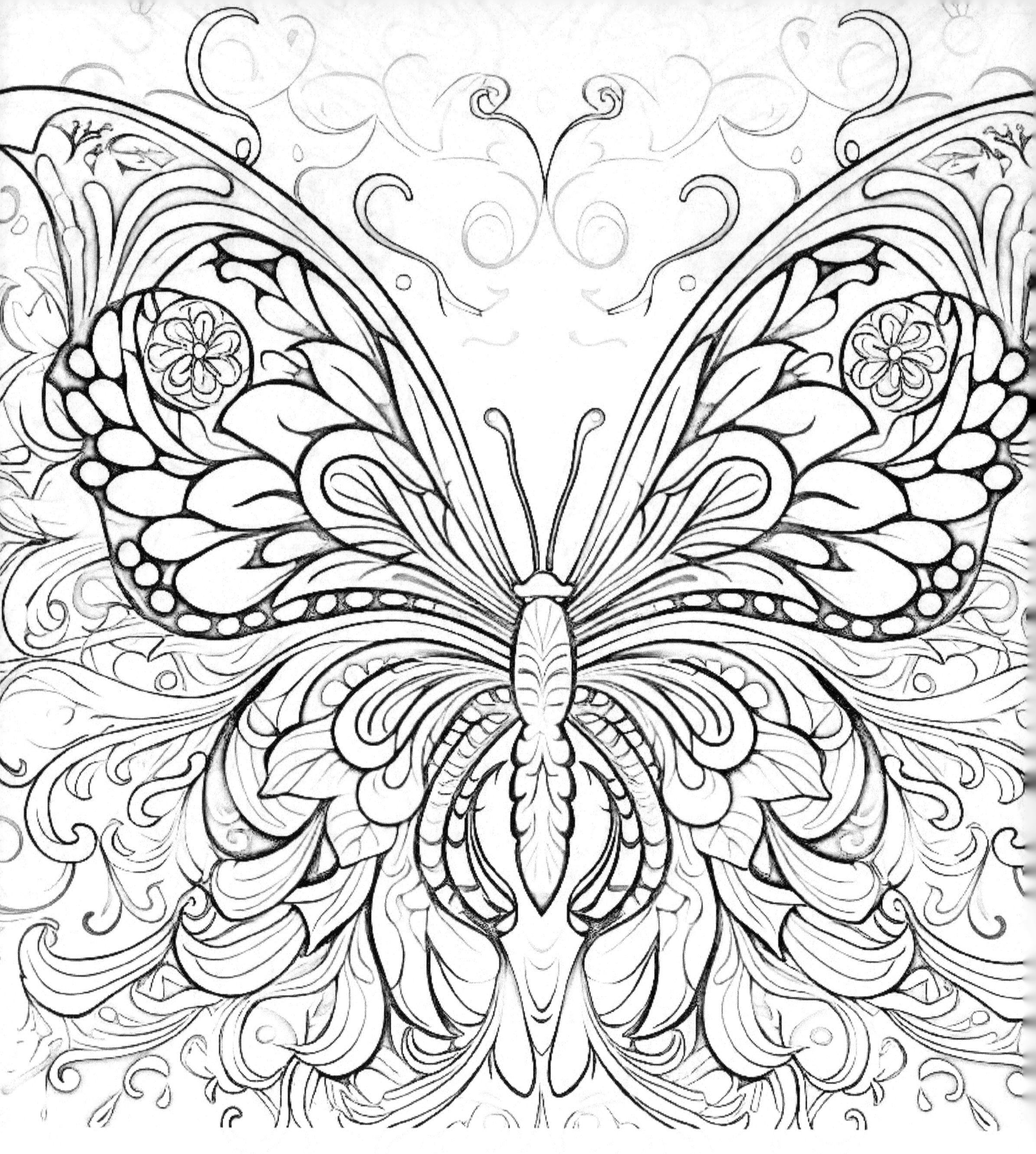

FREE

Constantly evolving, growing, and embracing transformation, I am free to fly wherever I choose.

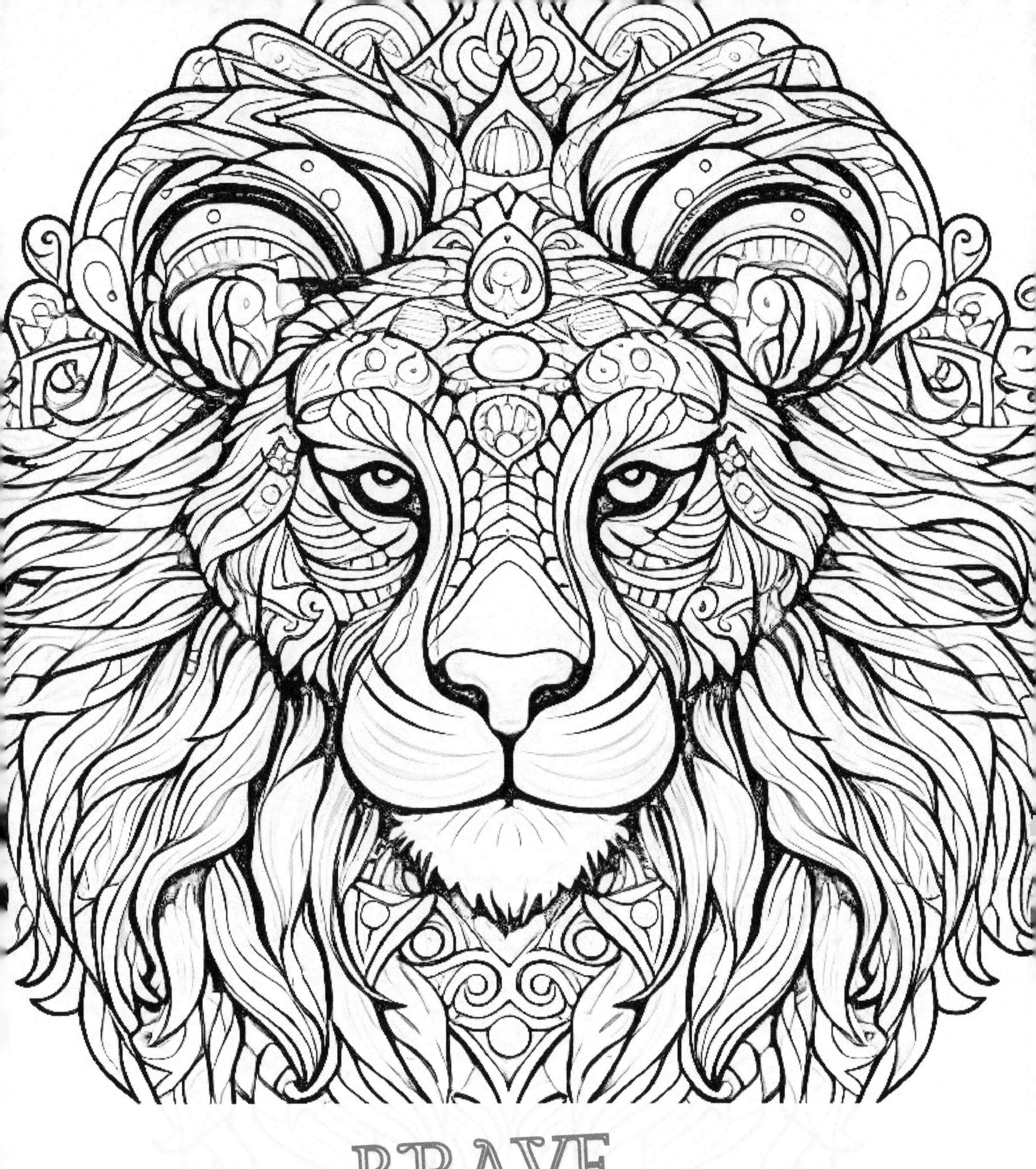

BRAVE

I am courageous and bold, fearlessly expressing my truth and standing my ground.

I glide gracefully through life's highs and lows, radiating calm and elegance.

GRACEFUL

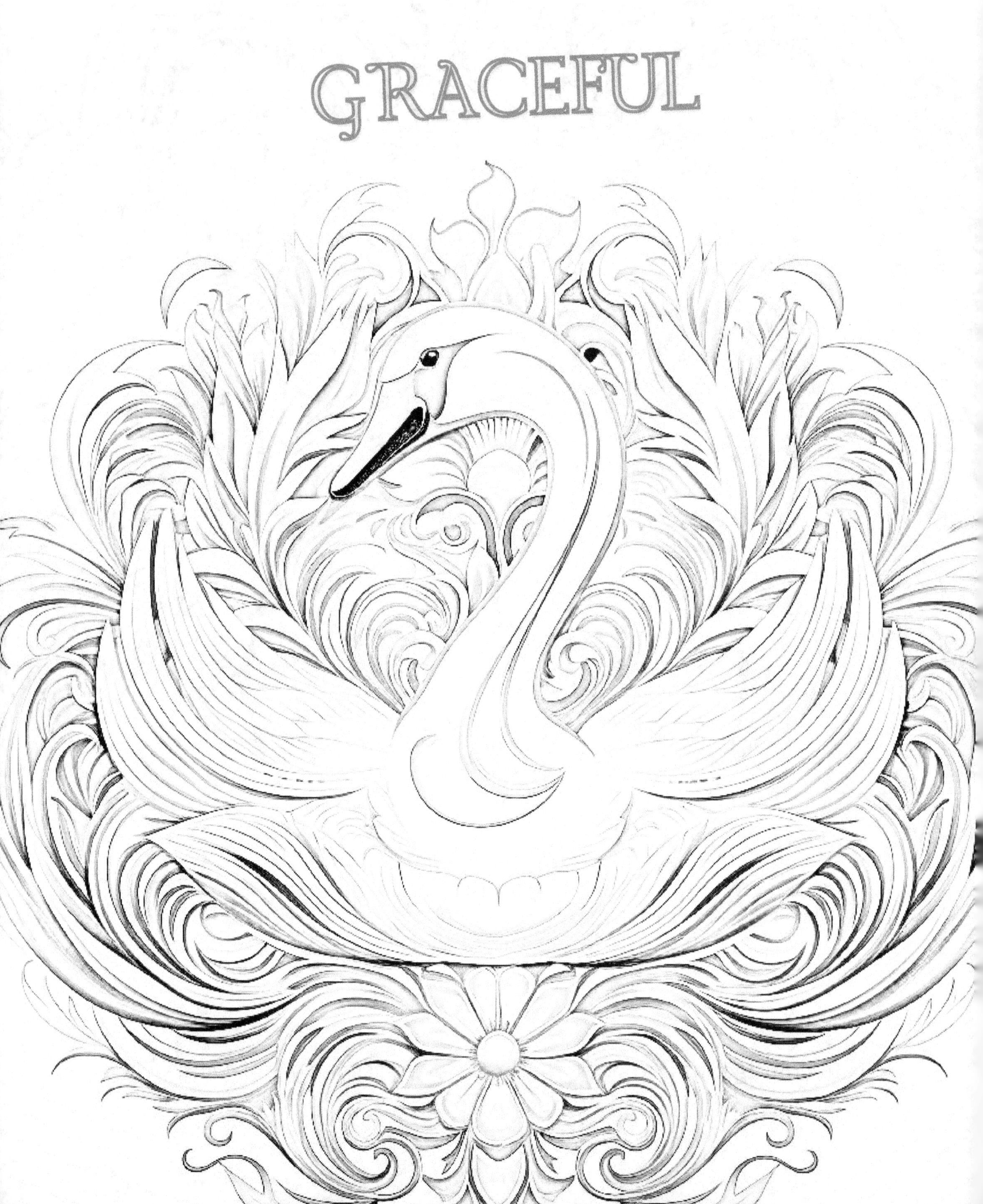

I am curious and love to explore. New experiences and joy in discovery are my driving forces.

ADVENTUROUS

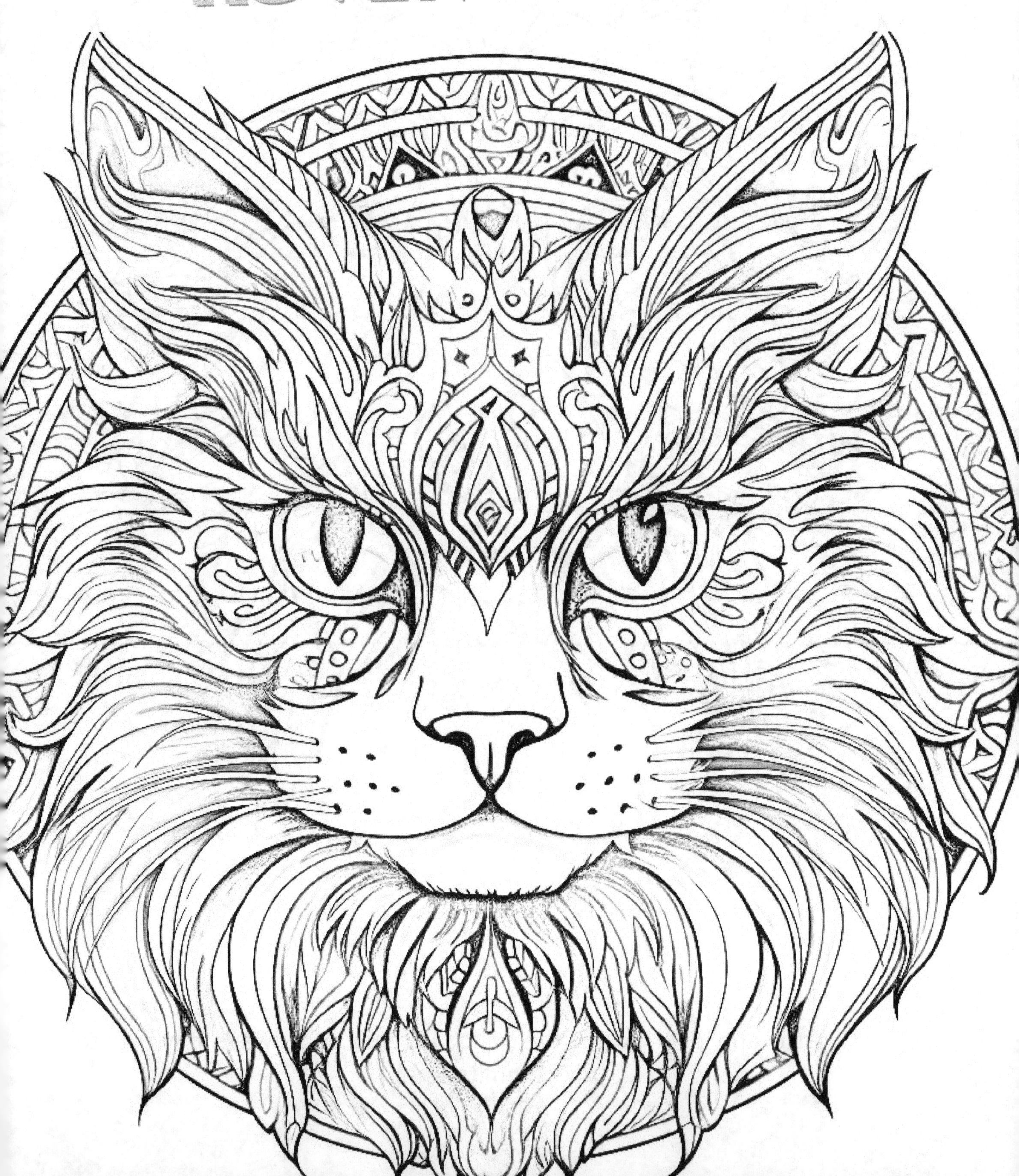

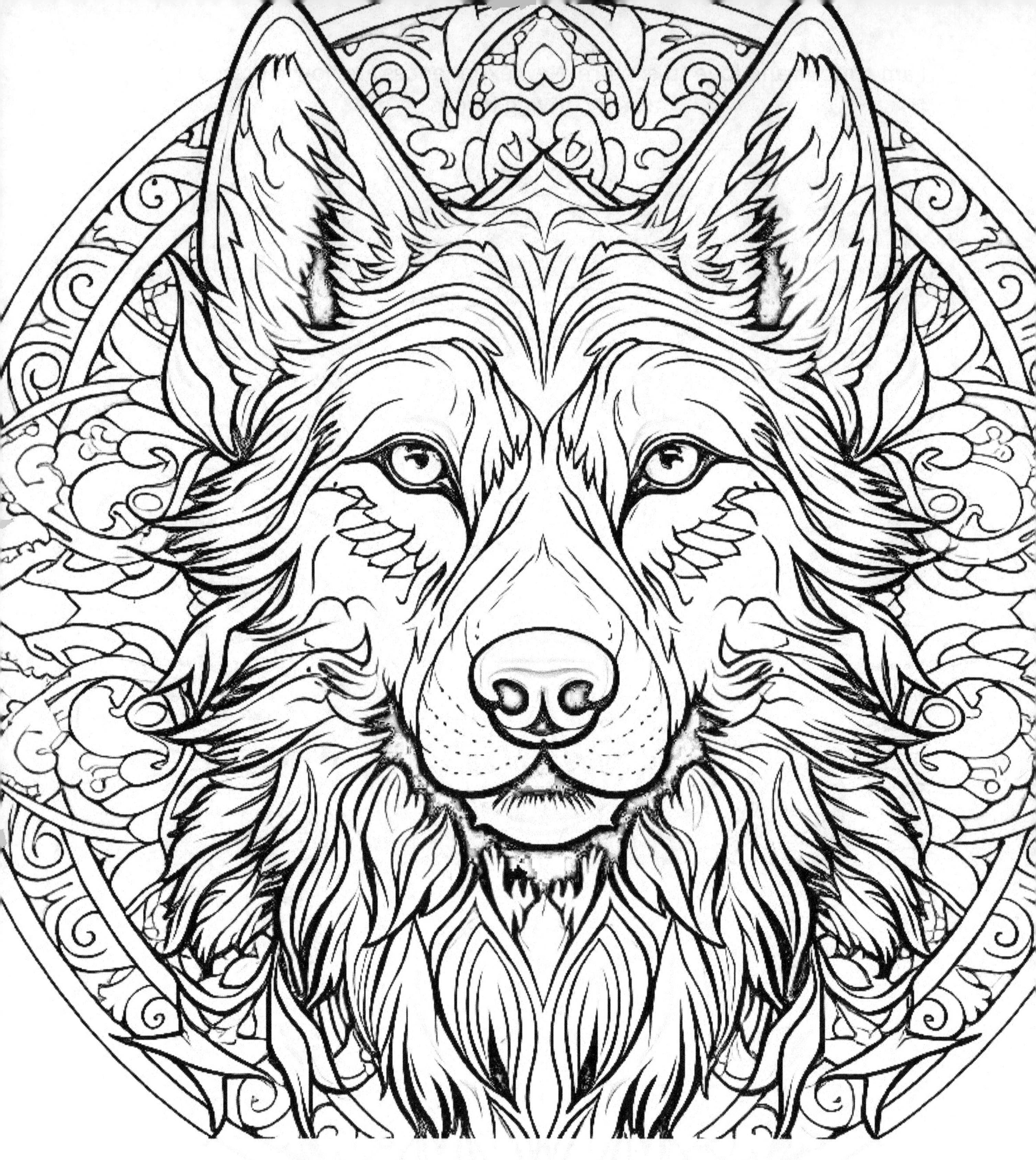

LOYAL

Trustworthy and loyal, I value the bonds I create and always stay true to my commitments.

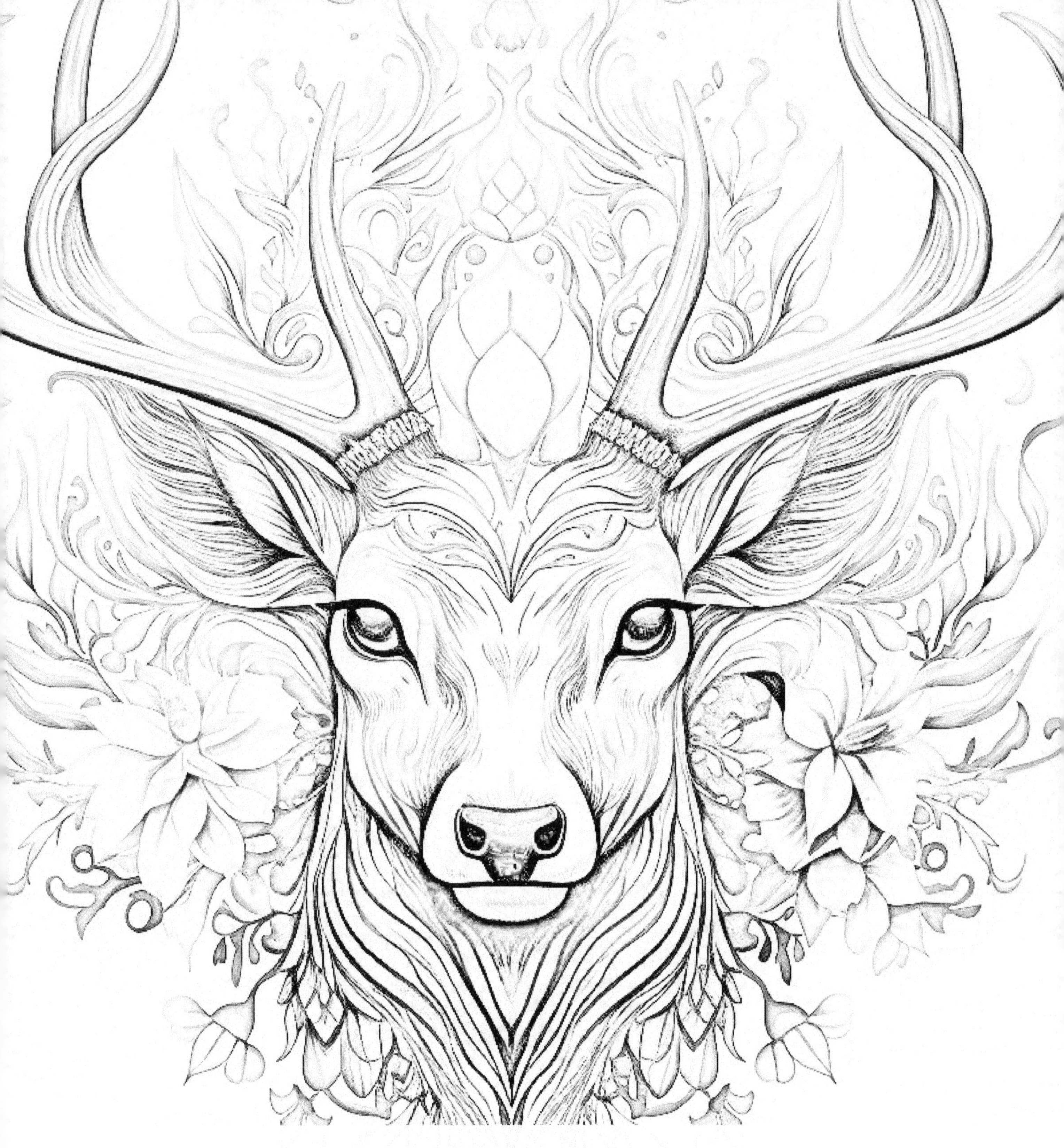

GENTLE

I move gently and quietly through life, leaving only good intentions in my wake.

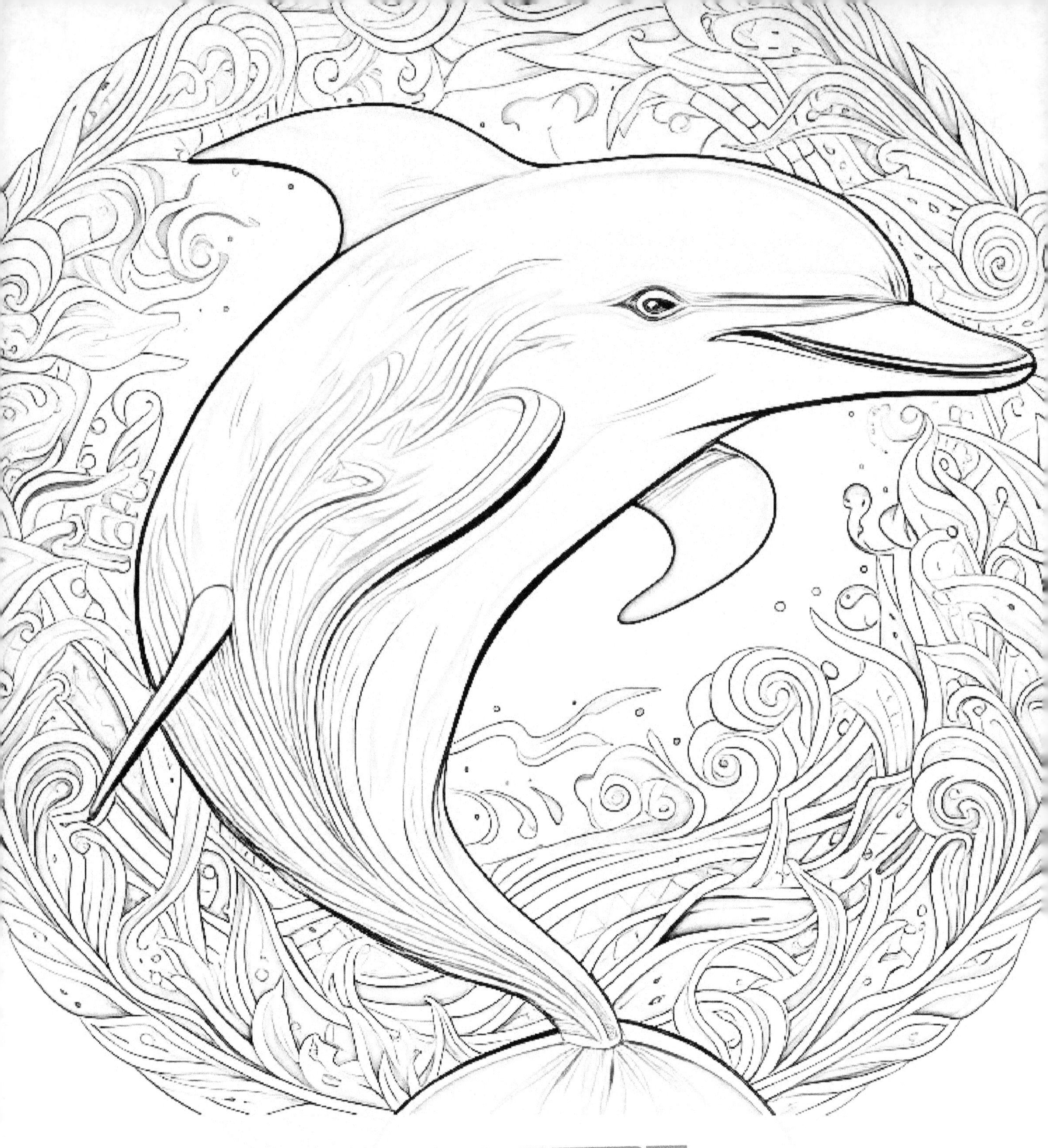

PLAYFUL

Embracing playfulness and joy, I celebrate life and spread positivity to those around me.

I am resilient, swimming upstream no matter what obstacles I face.

RESILIENT

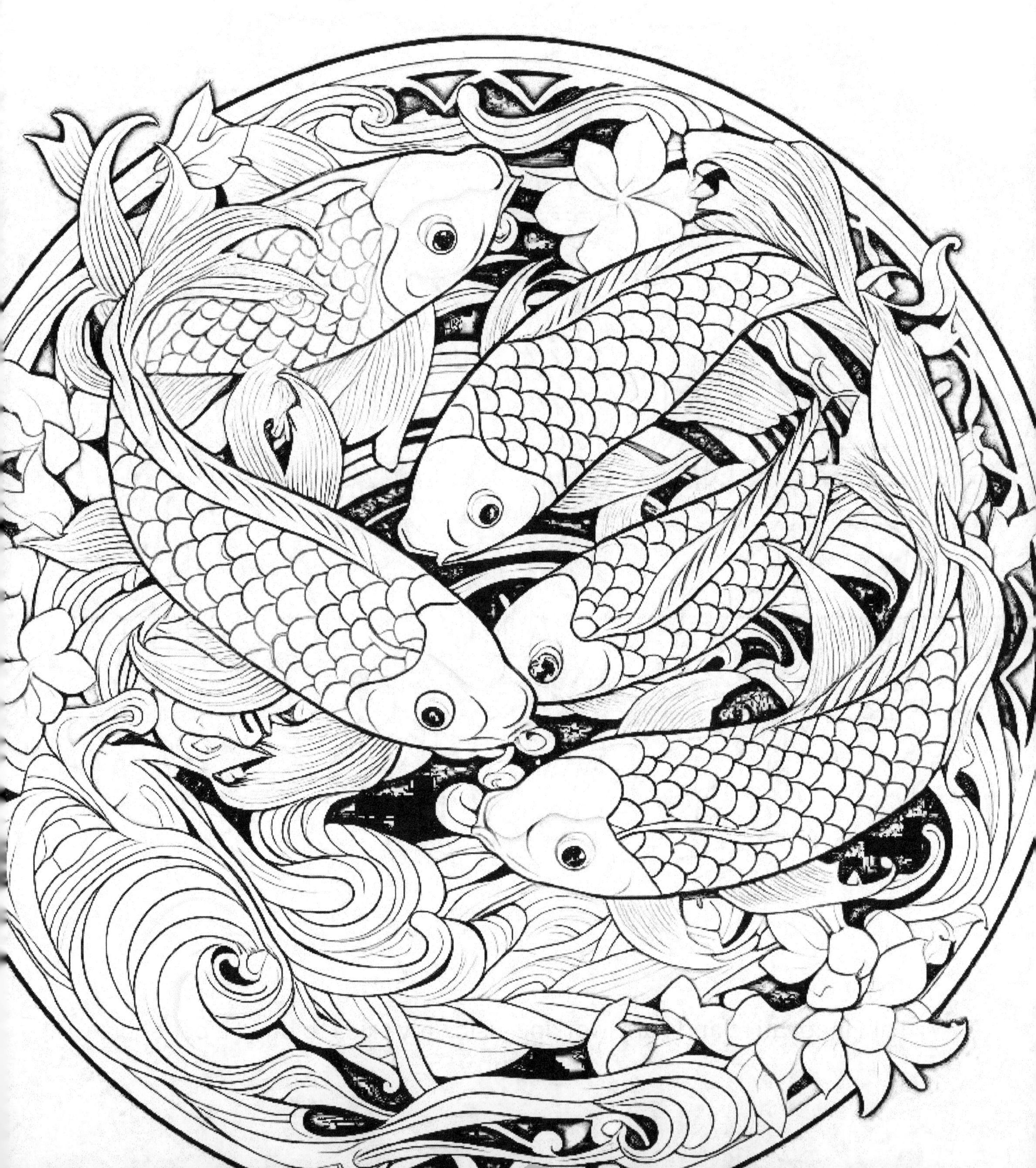

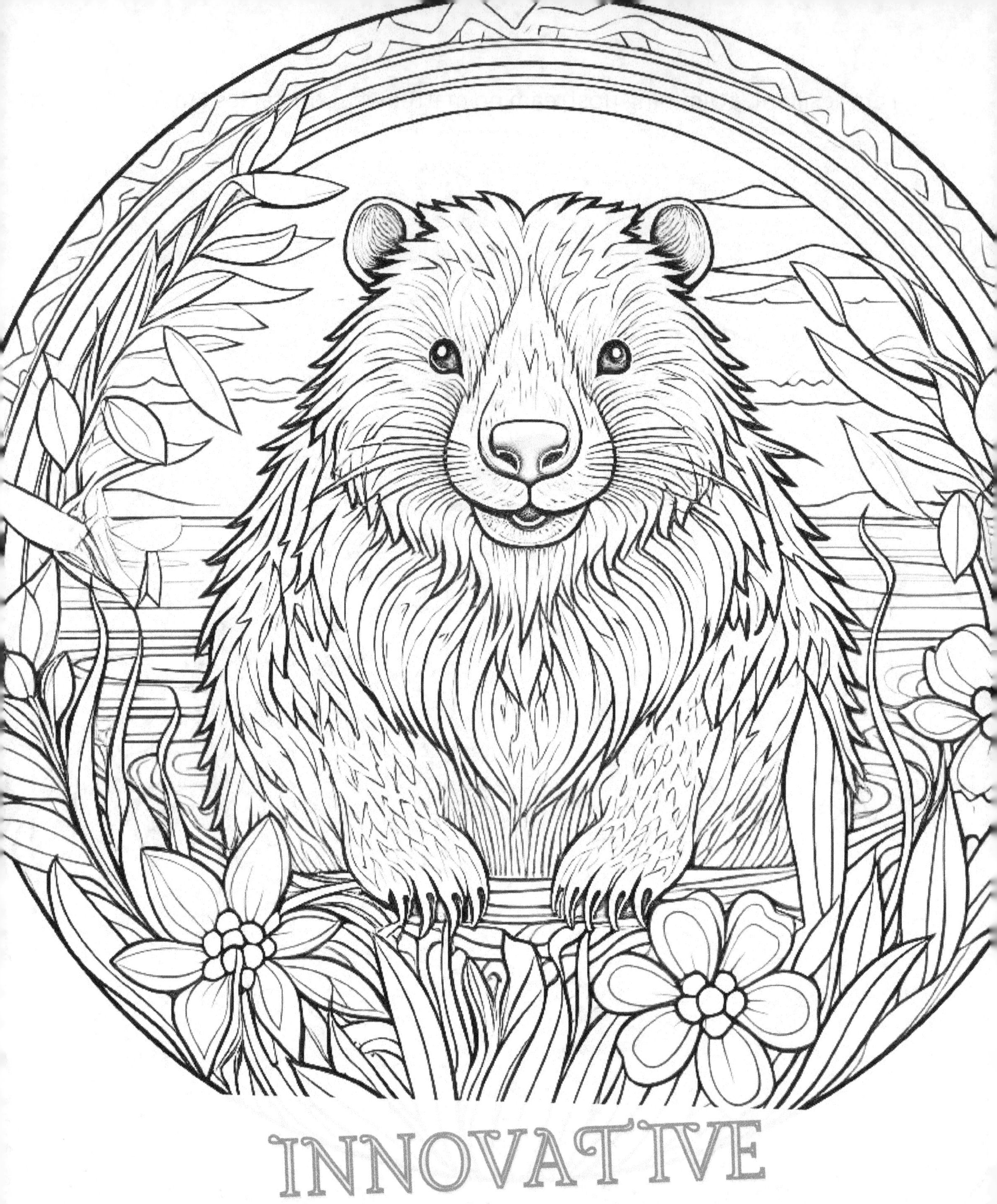

INNOVATIVE

I am innovative and hard-working, using my skills to build a beneficial future.

I value my solitude and take time for rest and introspection.

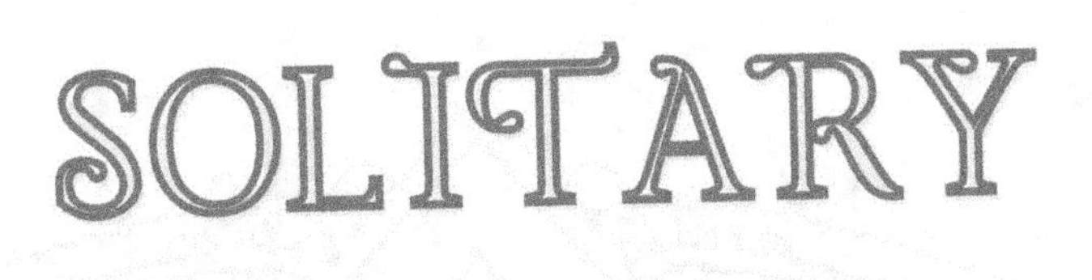

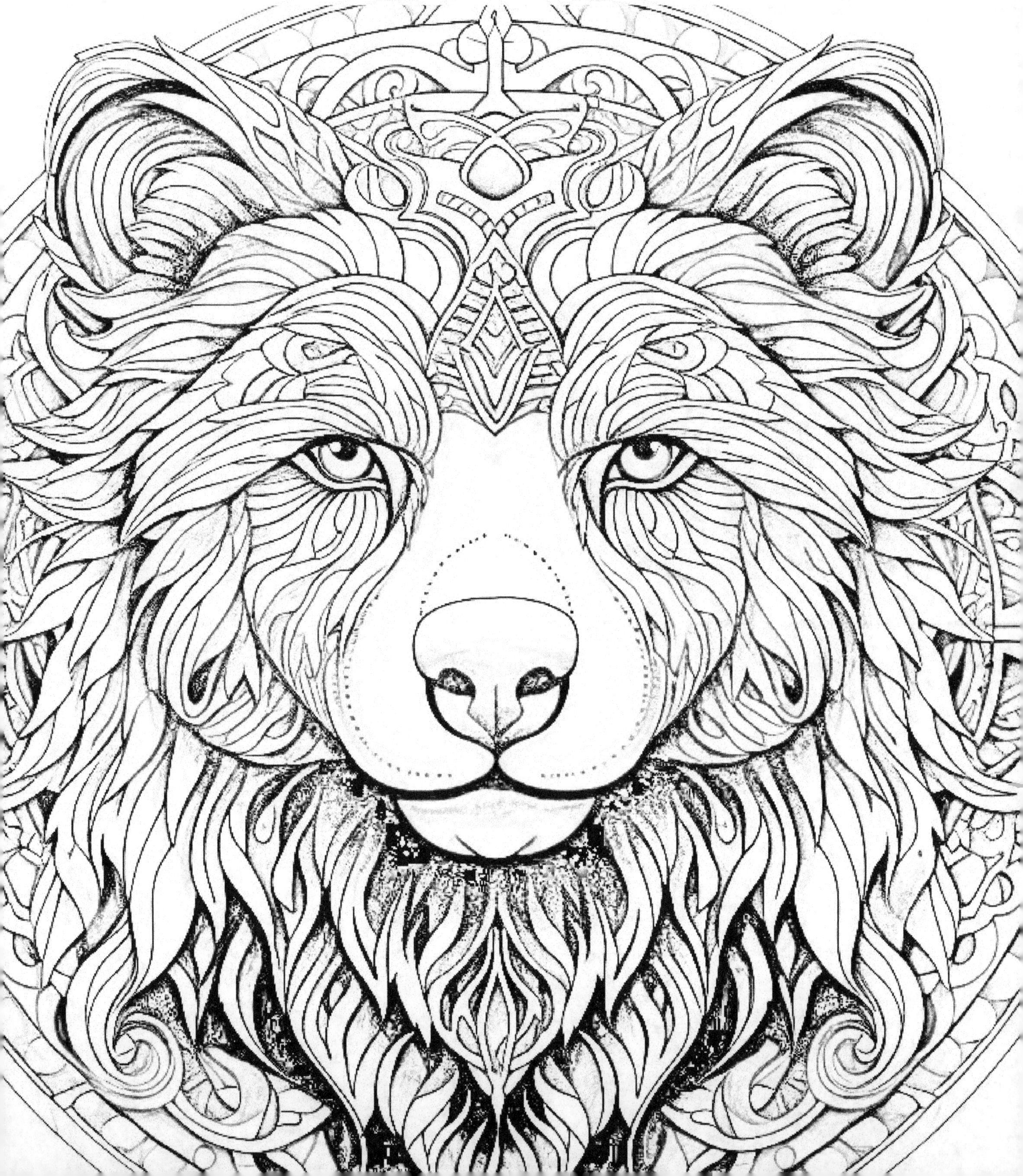

I rise above my challenges, soaring high and focusing on the bigger picture.

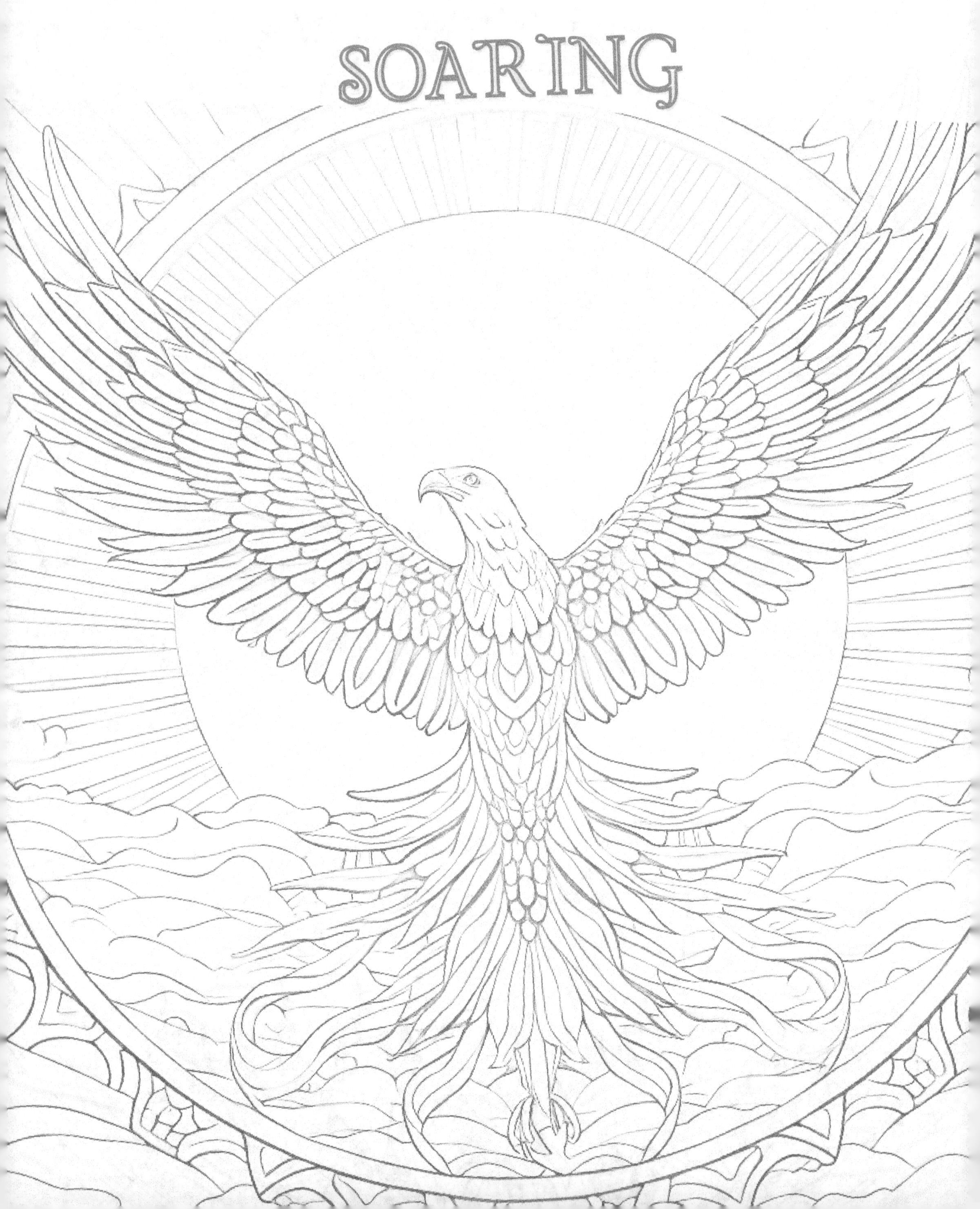

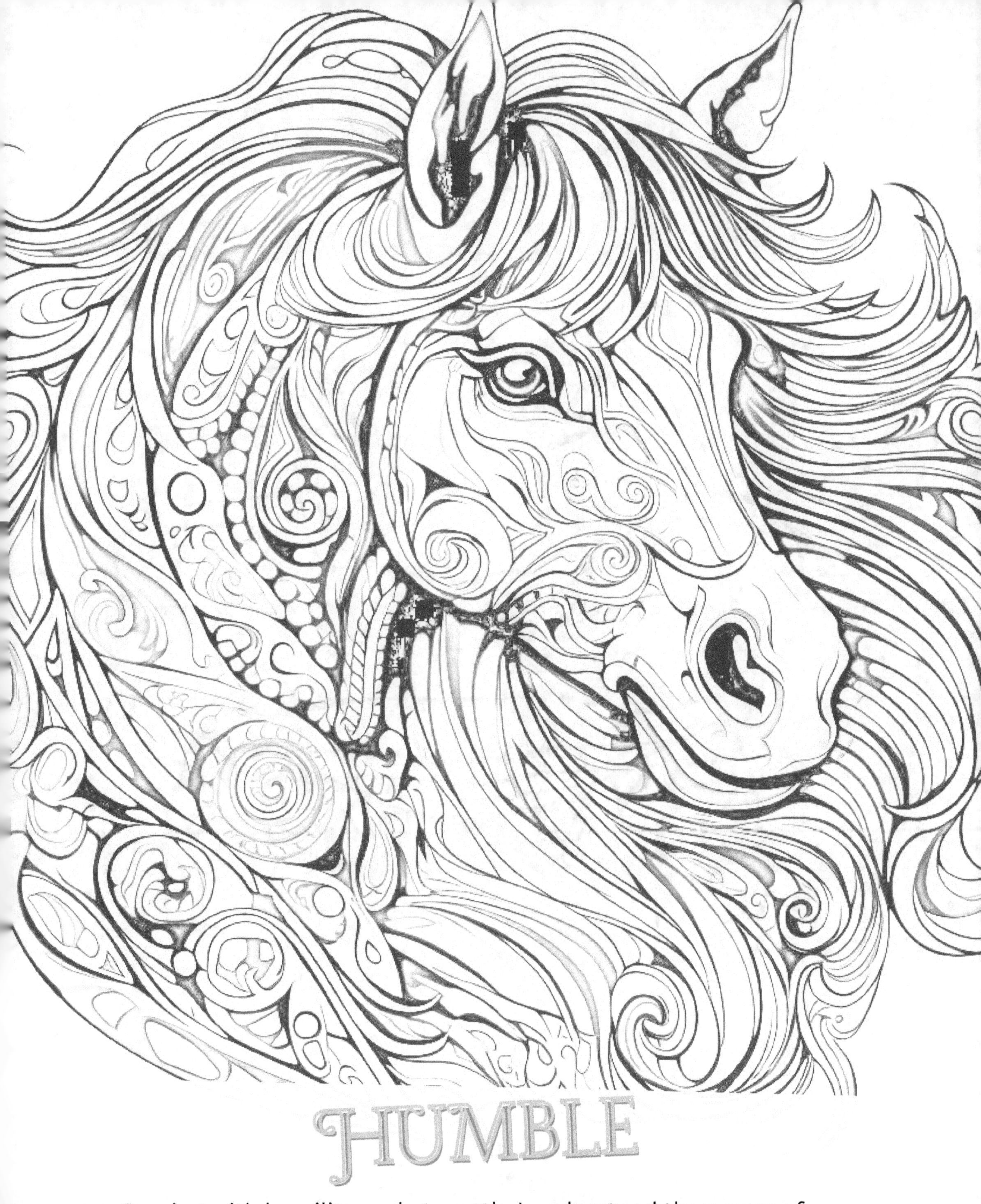

HUMBLE

Serving with humility and strength, I understand the power of teamwork and cooperation.

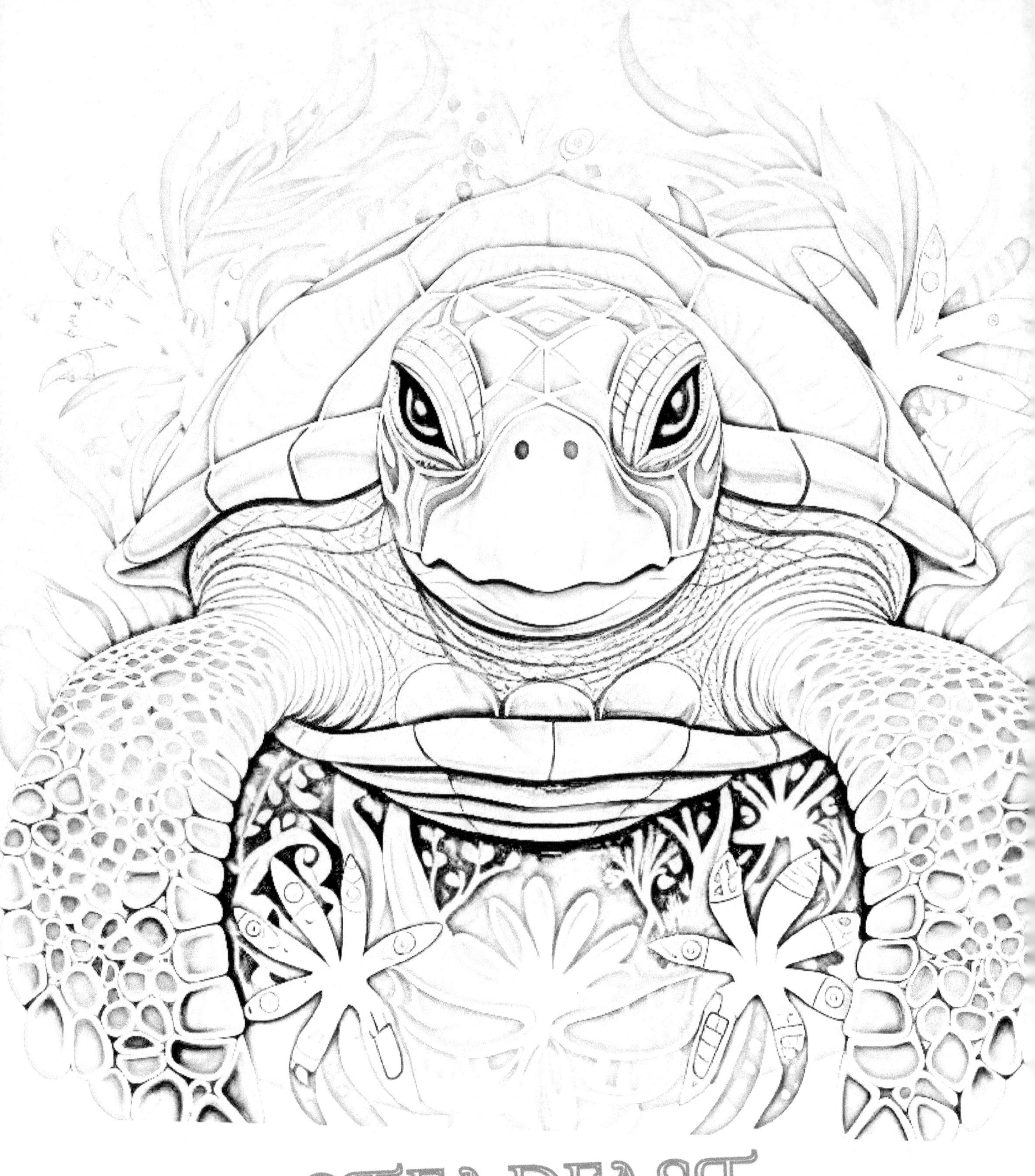

STEADFAST

I am patient and persistent, knowing that progress may be slow, but the journey is worth it.

I adapt to changes with ease and remain true to myself in any situation.

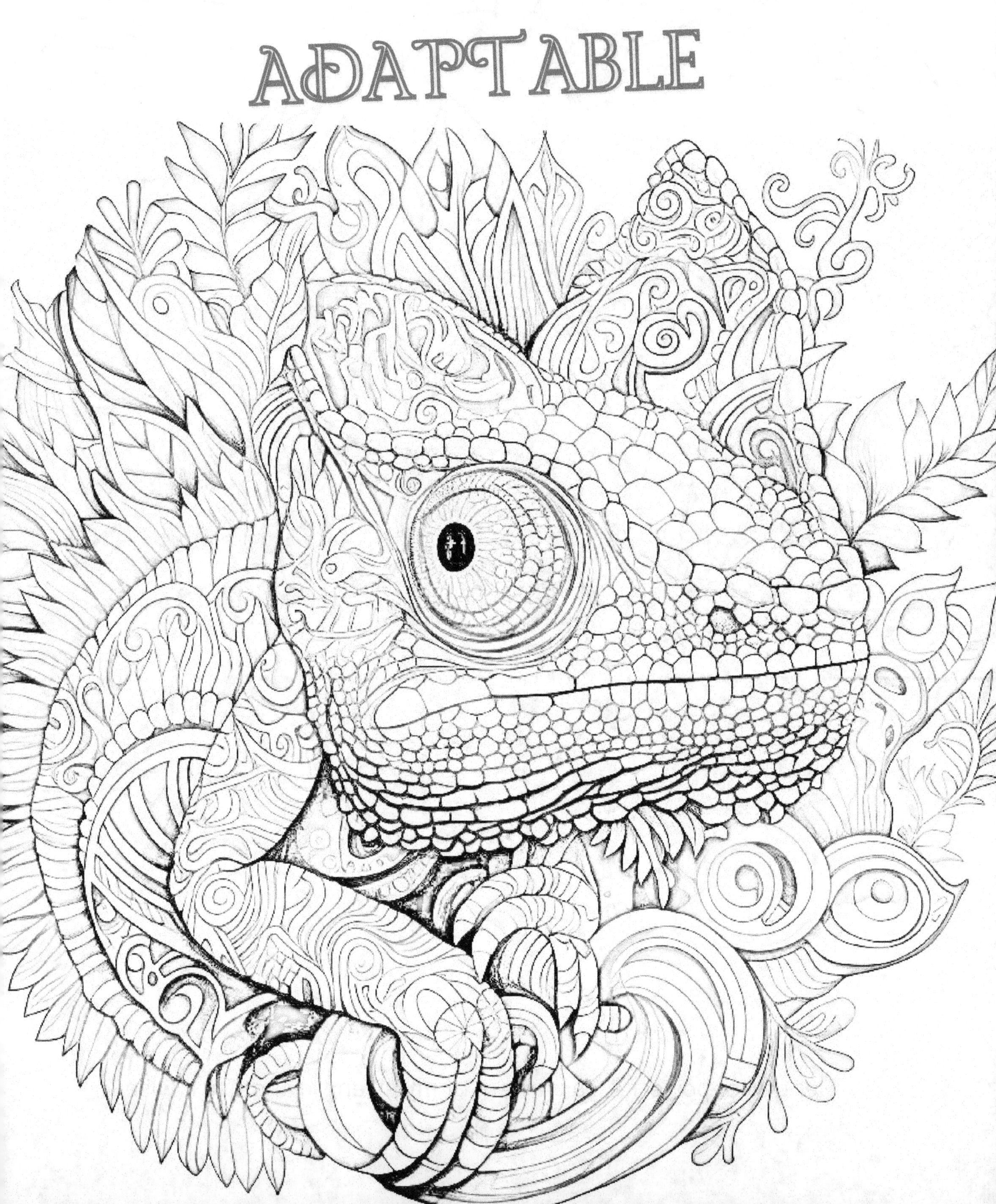

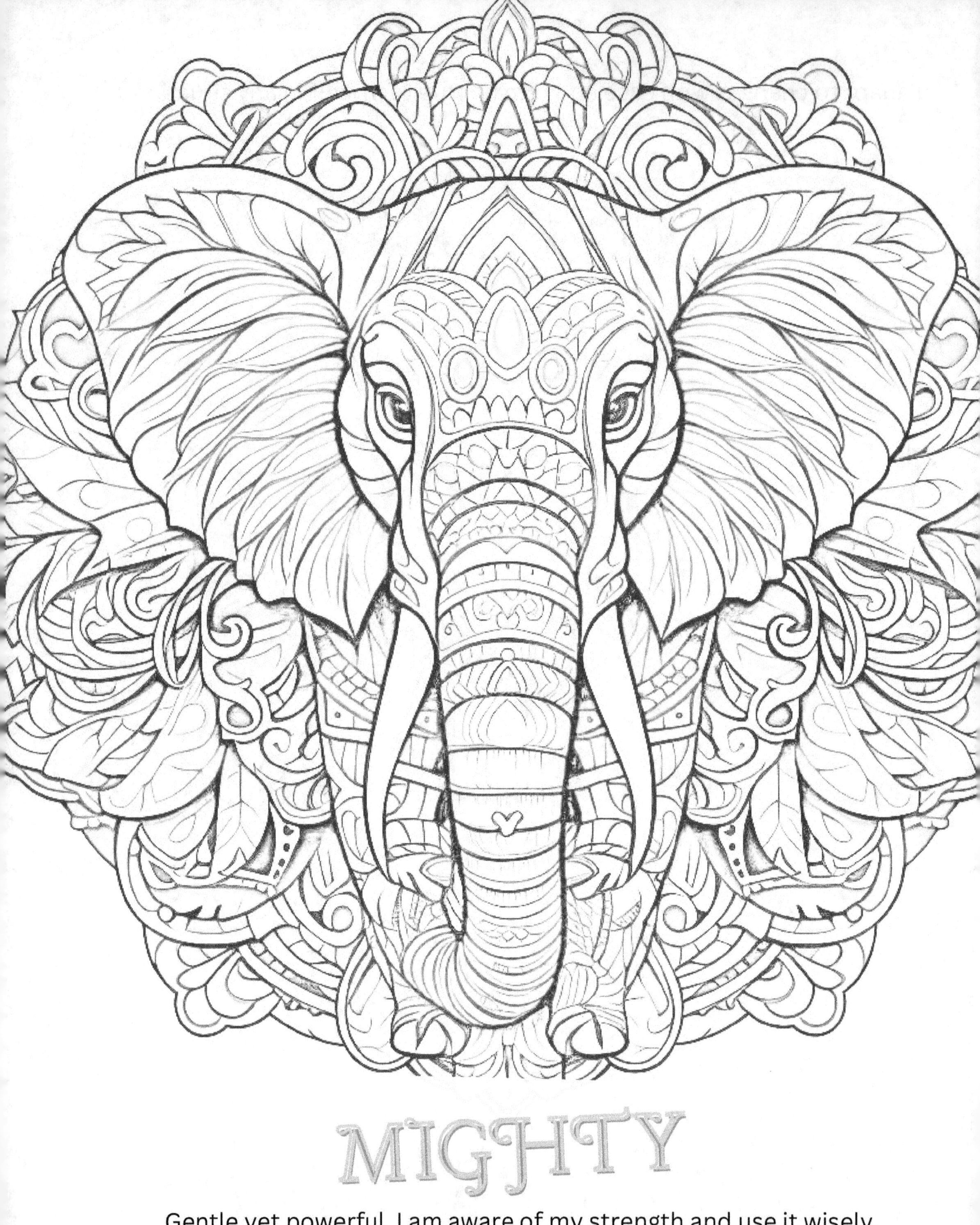

MIGHTY

Gentle yet powerful, I am aware of my strength and use it wisely.

I stay grounded in my principles, respecting nature and understanding the cycle of life.

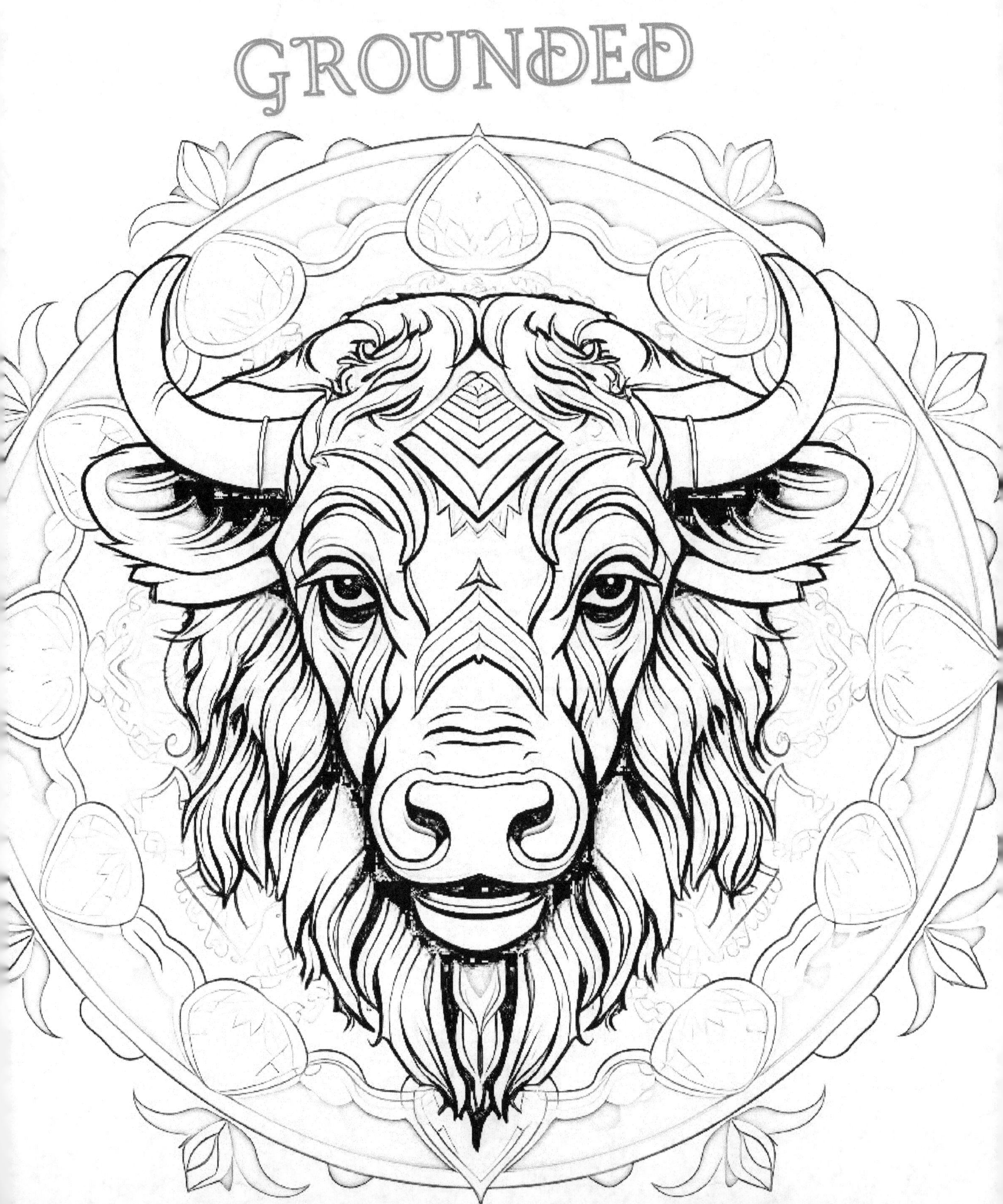

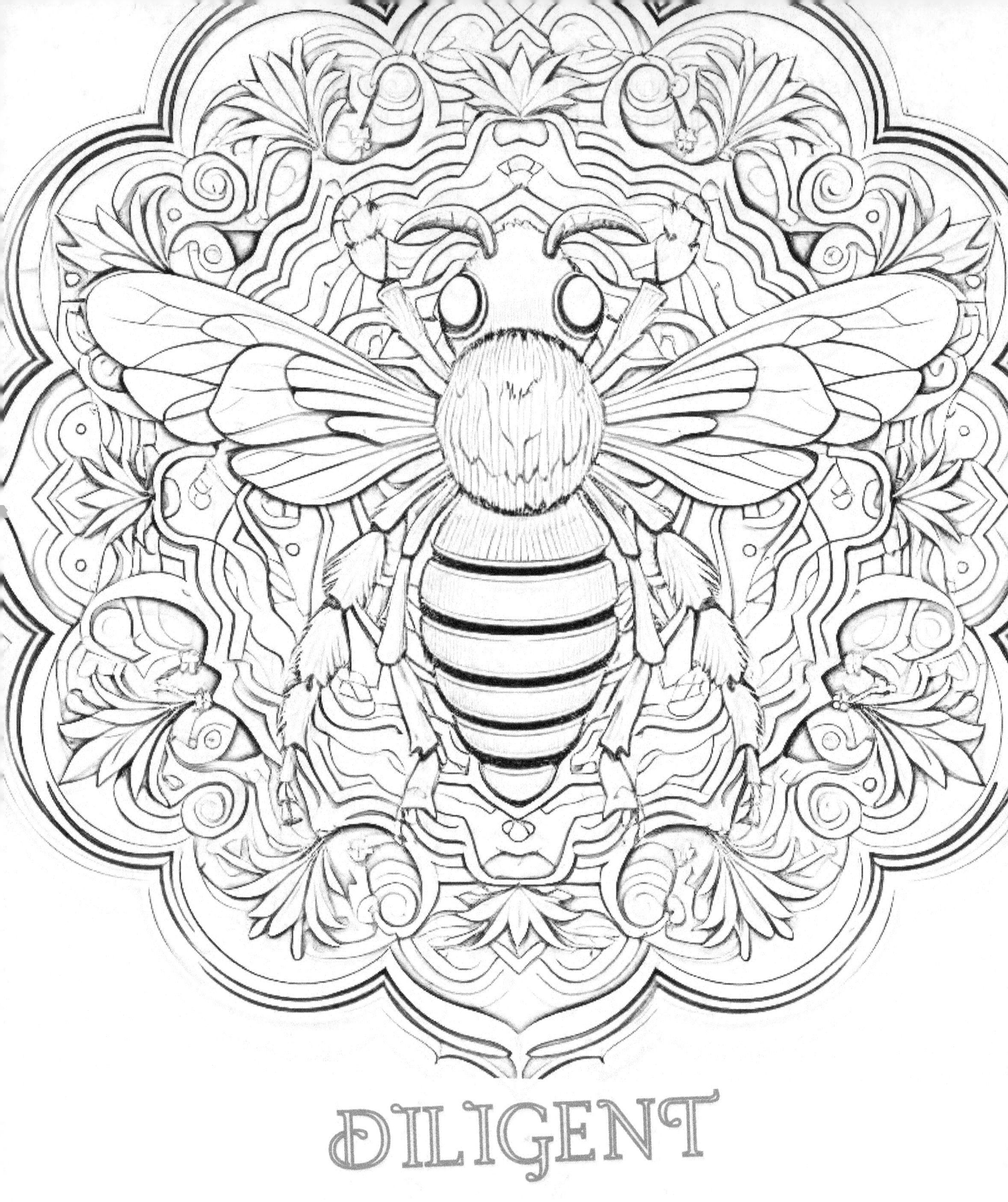

DILIGENT

I am diligent and productive, knowing that my hard work contributes to a larger purpose.

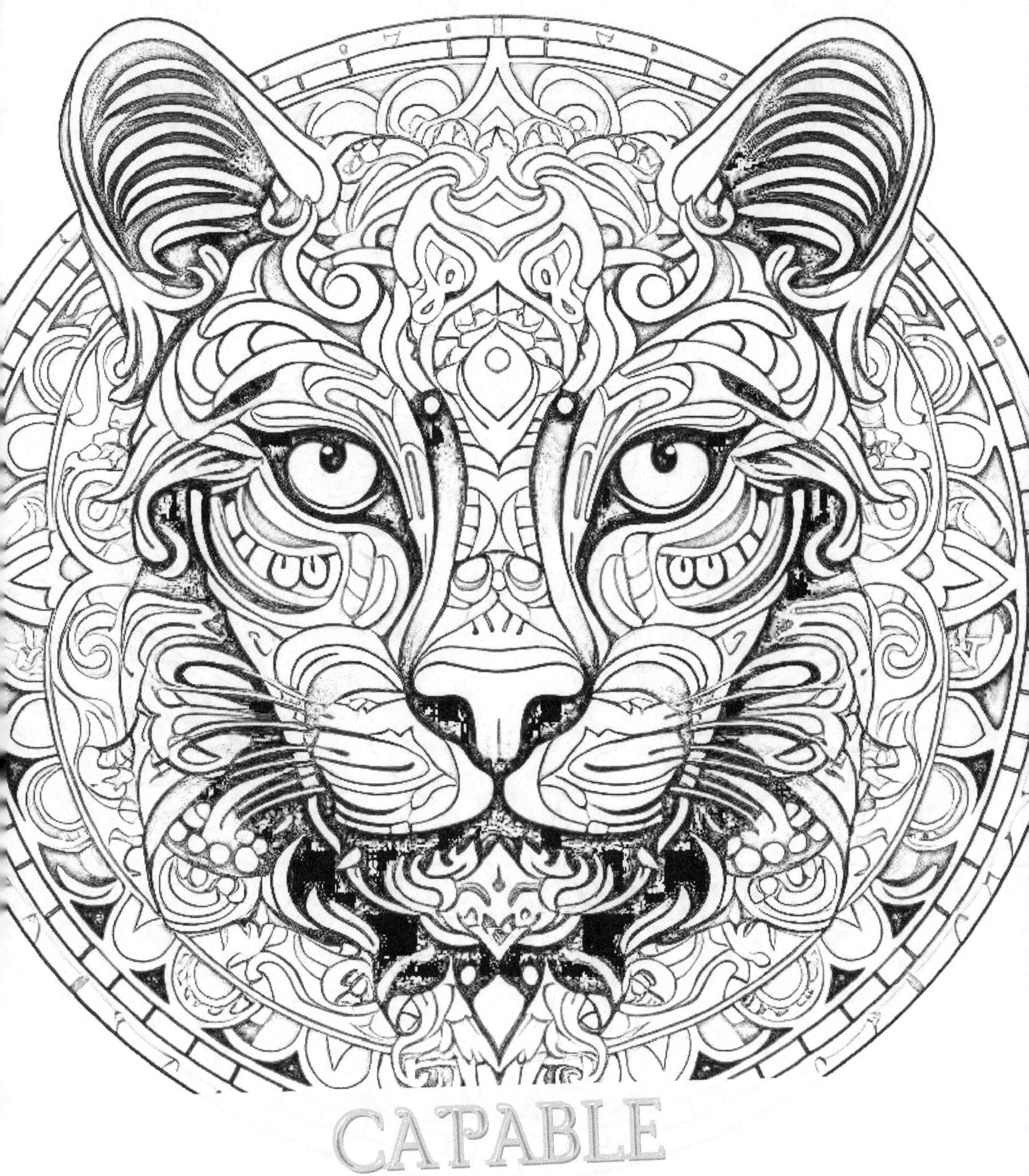

CAPABLE

I am capable and comfortable with solitude, cherishing my time alone for self-reflection and growth.

I live in the moment and savor the nectar of life, full of energy and enthusiasm.

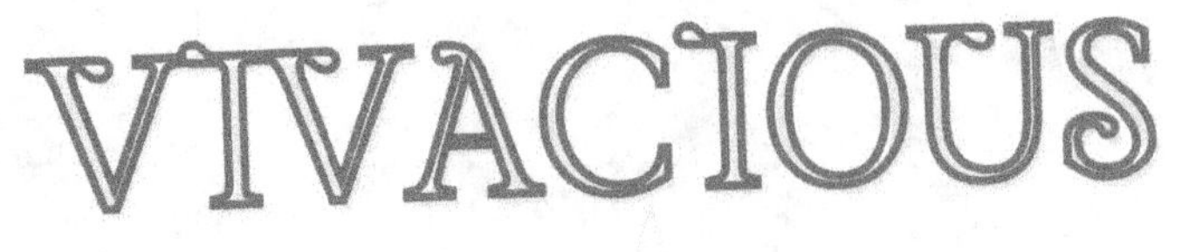

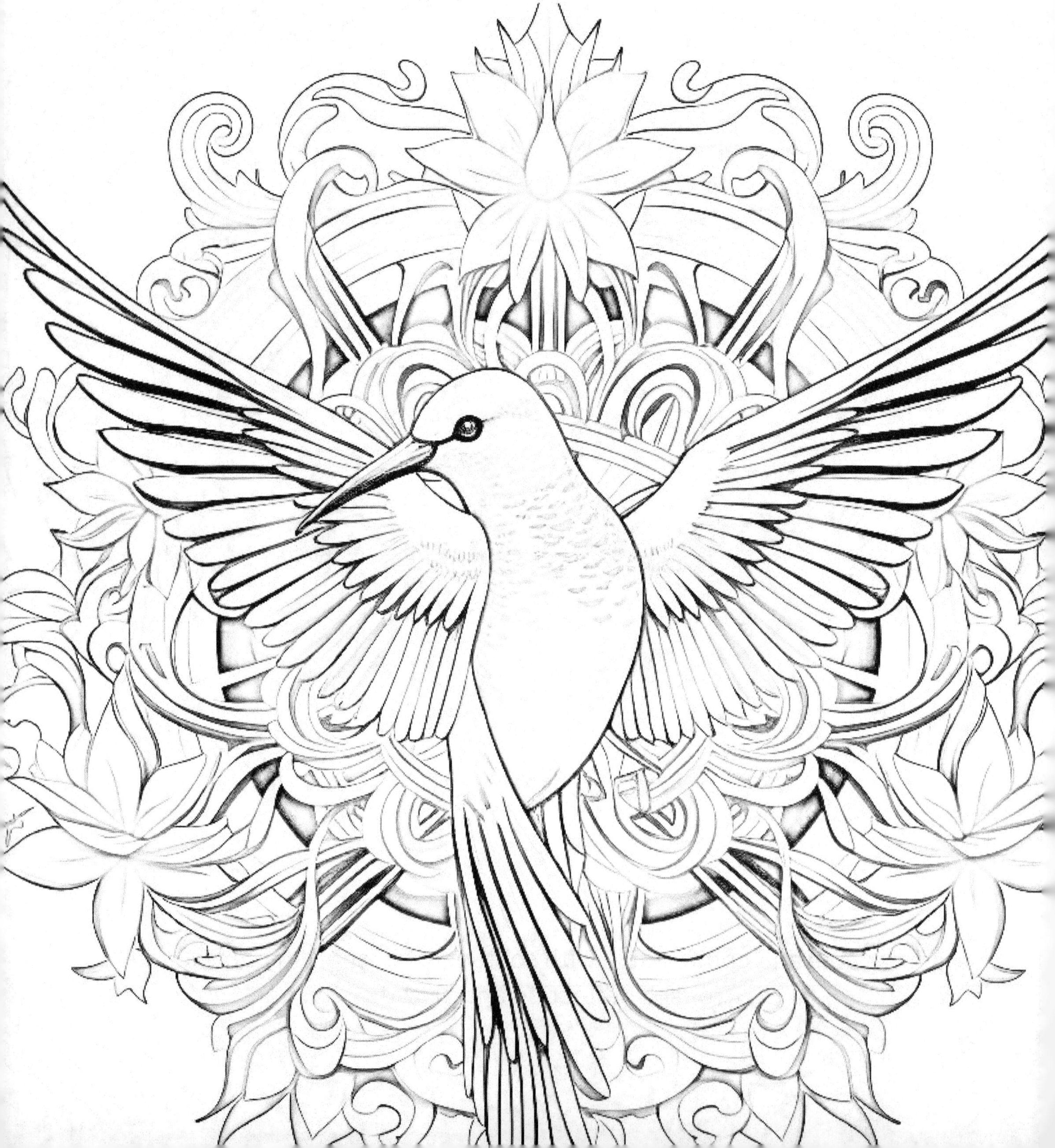

I am proud of who I am and I shine my light brightly.

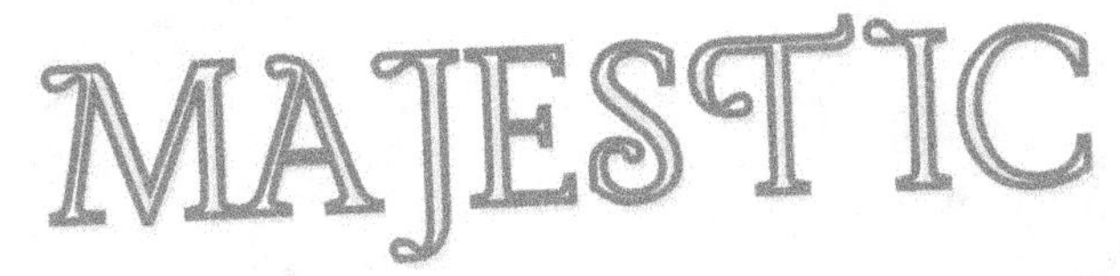

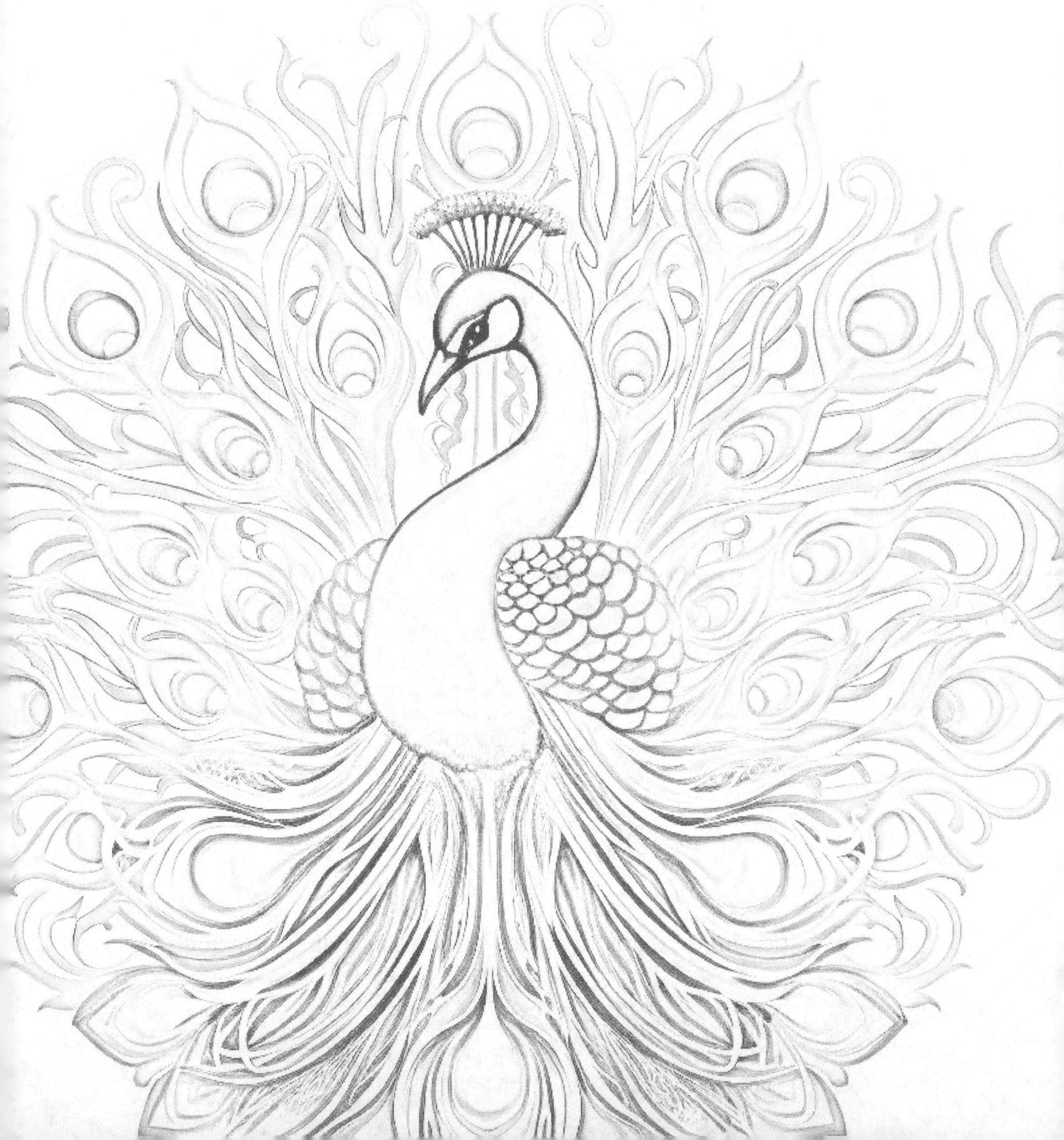

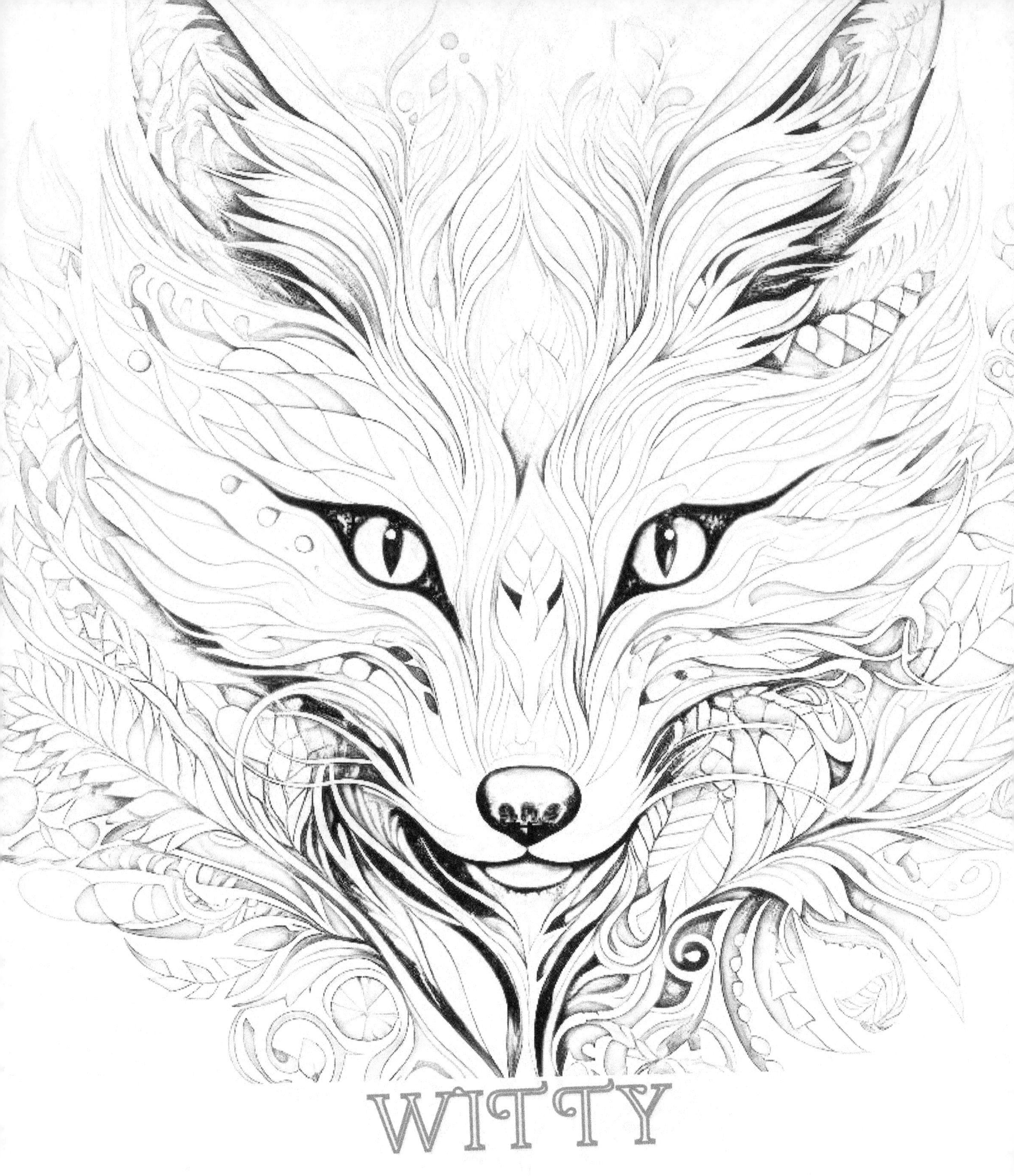

WITTY

I am witty and clever, using my intelligence to navigate through life's complexities.

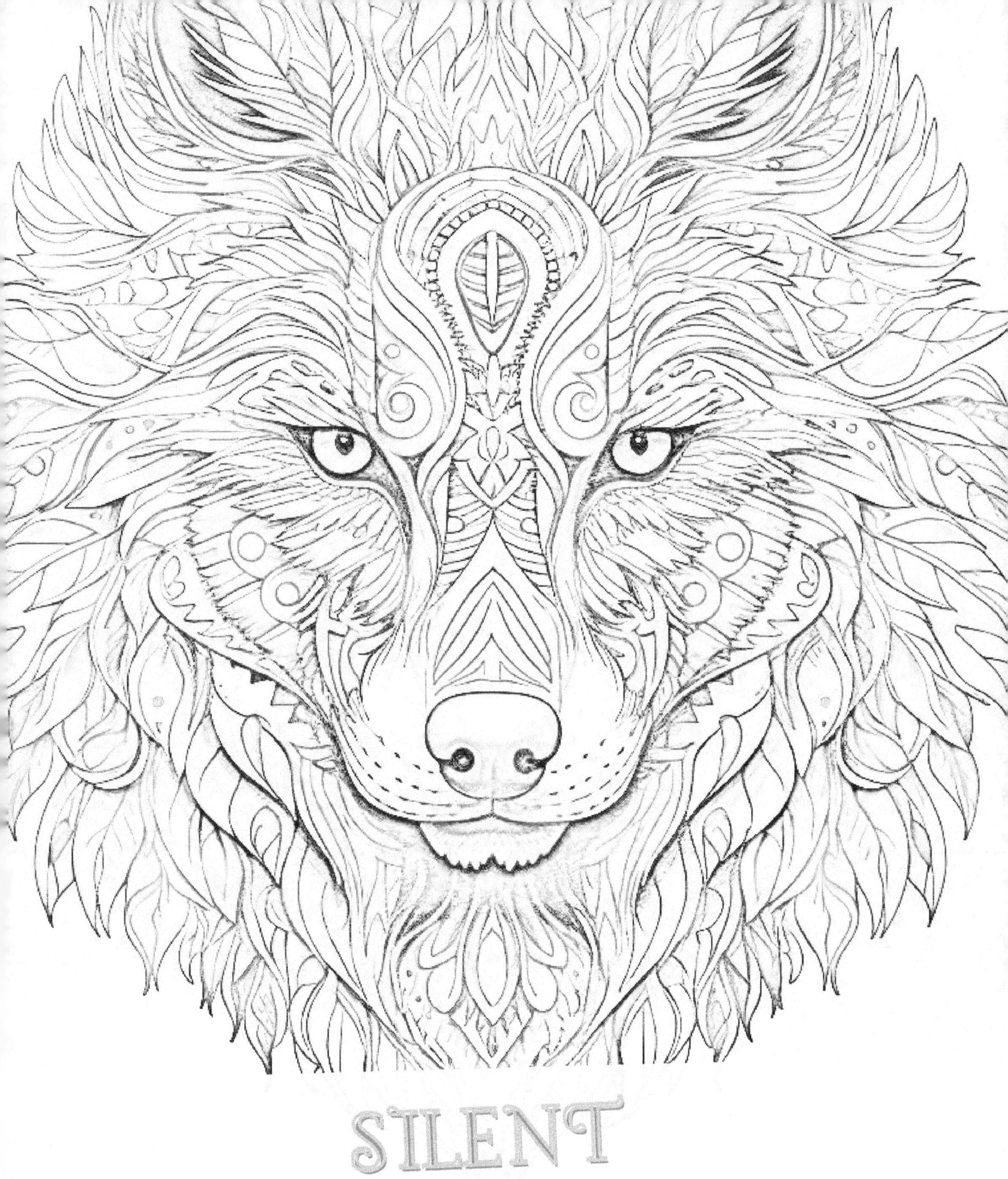

SILENT

I am a silent observer and a strong communicator, listening before speaking and understanding the power of words.

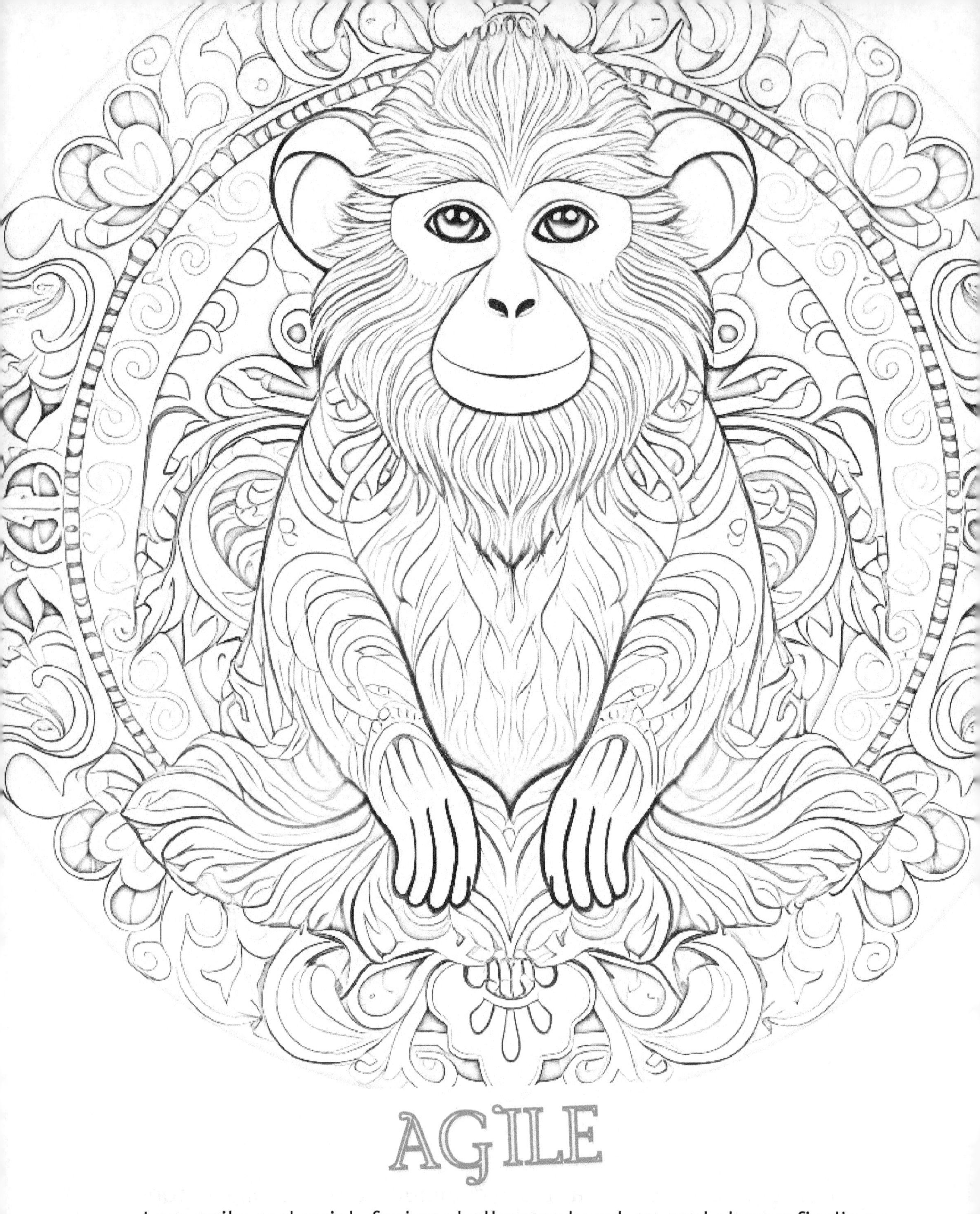

AGILE

I am agile and quick, facing challenges head-on and always finding a way forward.

I am peaceful and calm, seeking harmony in all things and believing in the power of love.

PEACEFUL

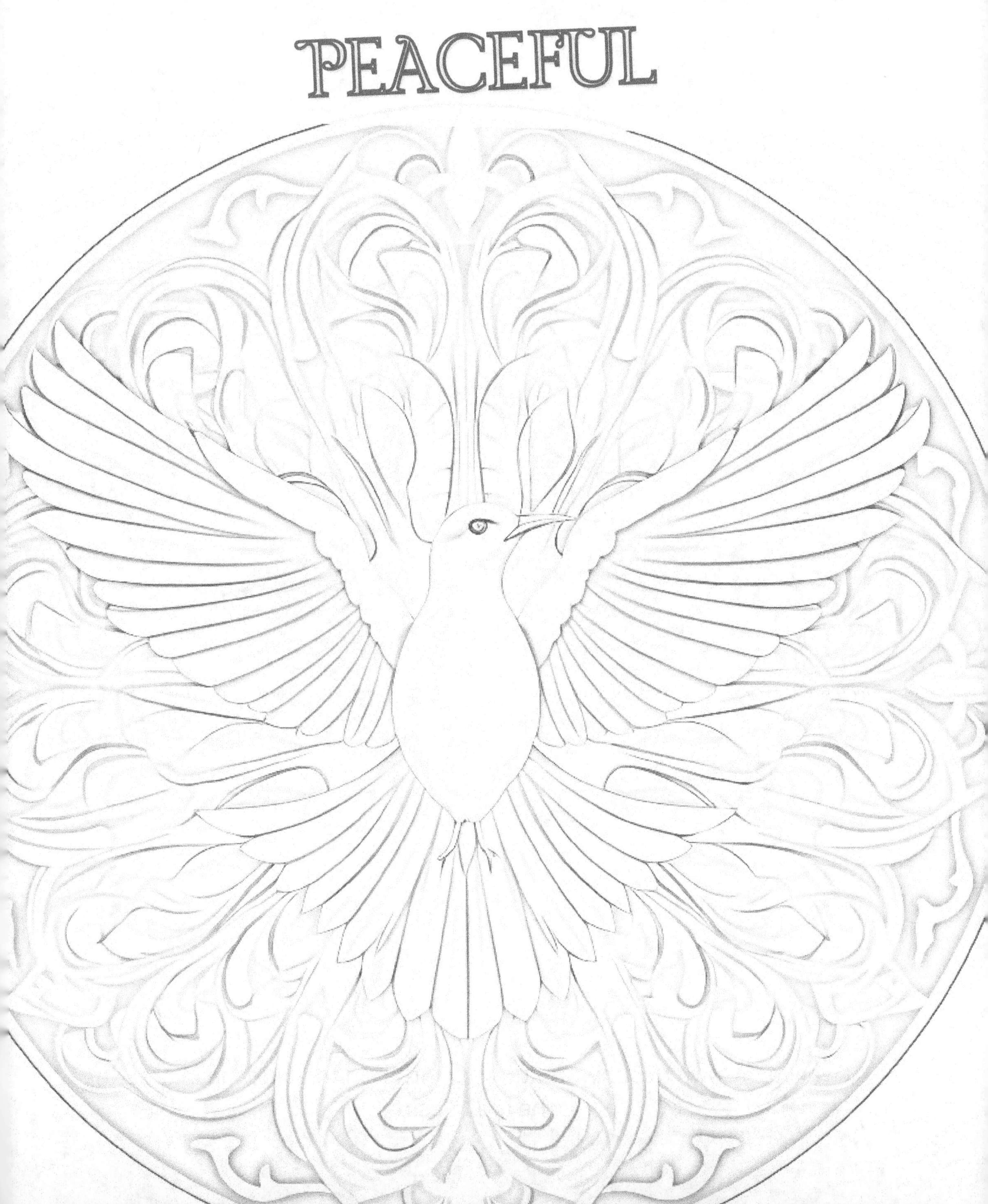

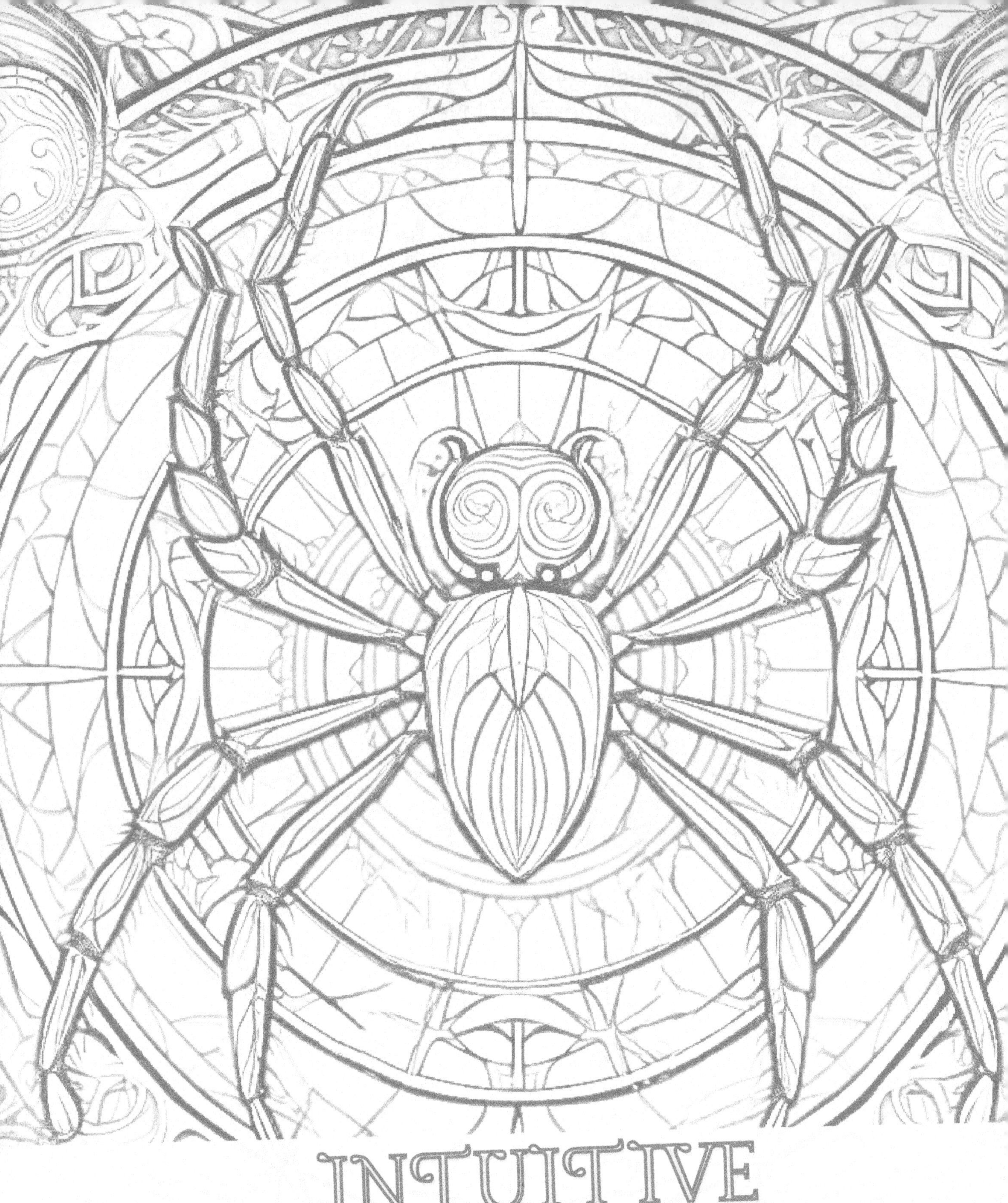

INTUITIVE

I weave my own destiny, trusting my intuition to guide me in creating the life I desire.

I move quickly towards my goals, seizing opportunities and making the most of my time.

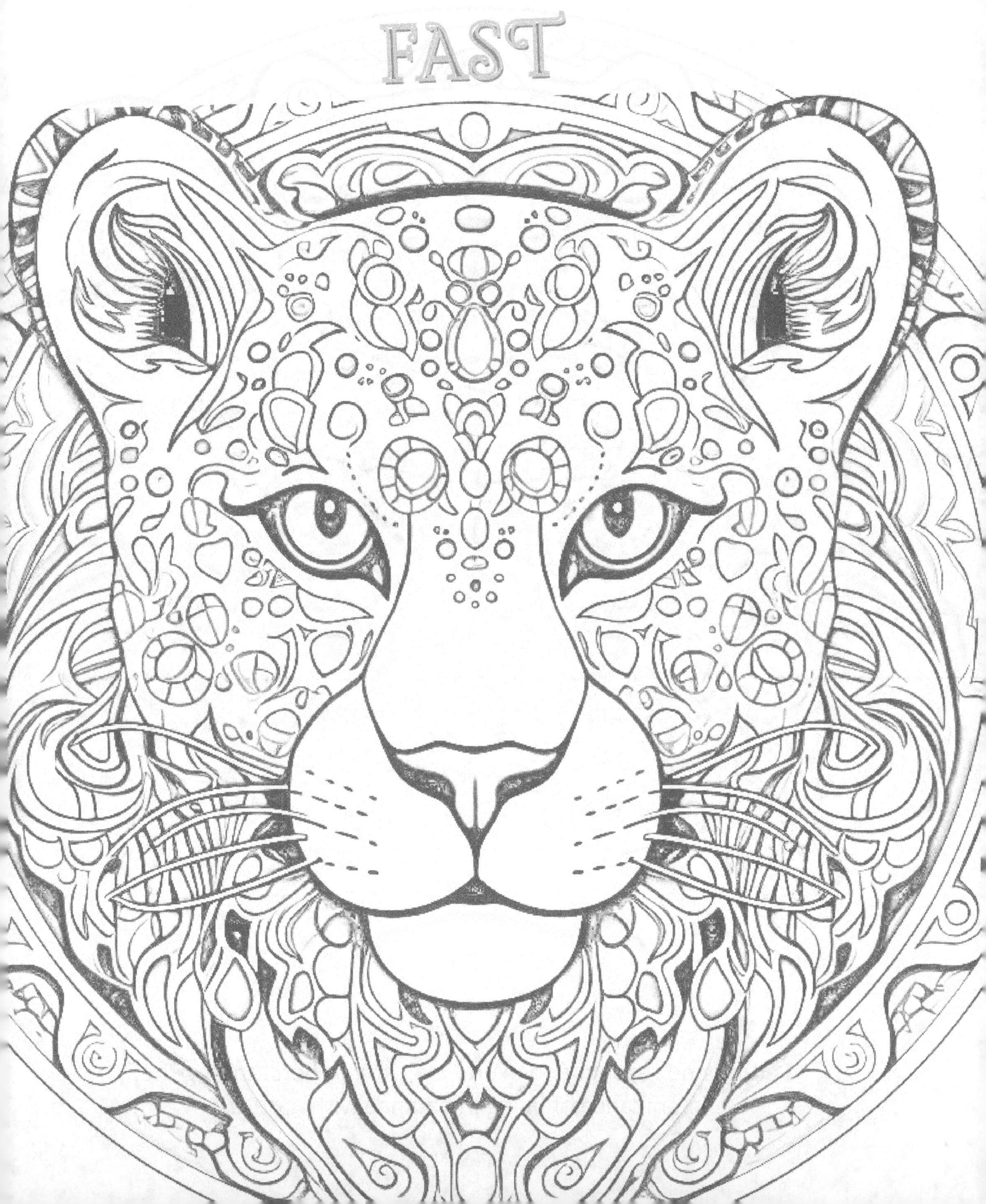

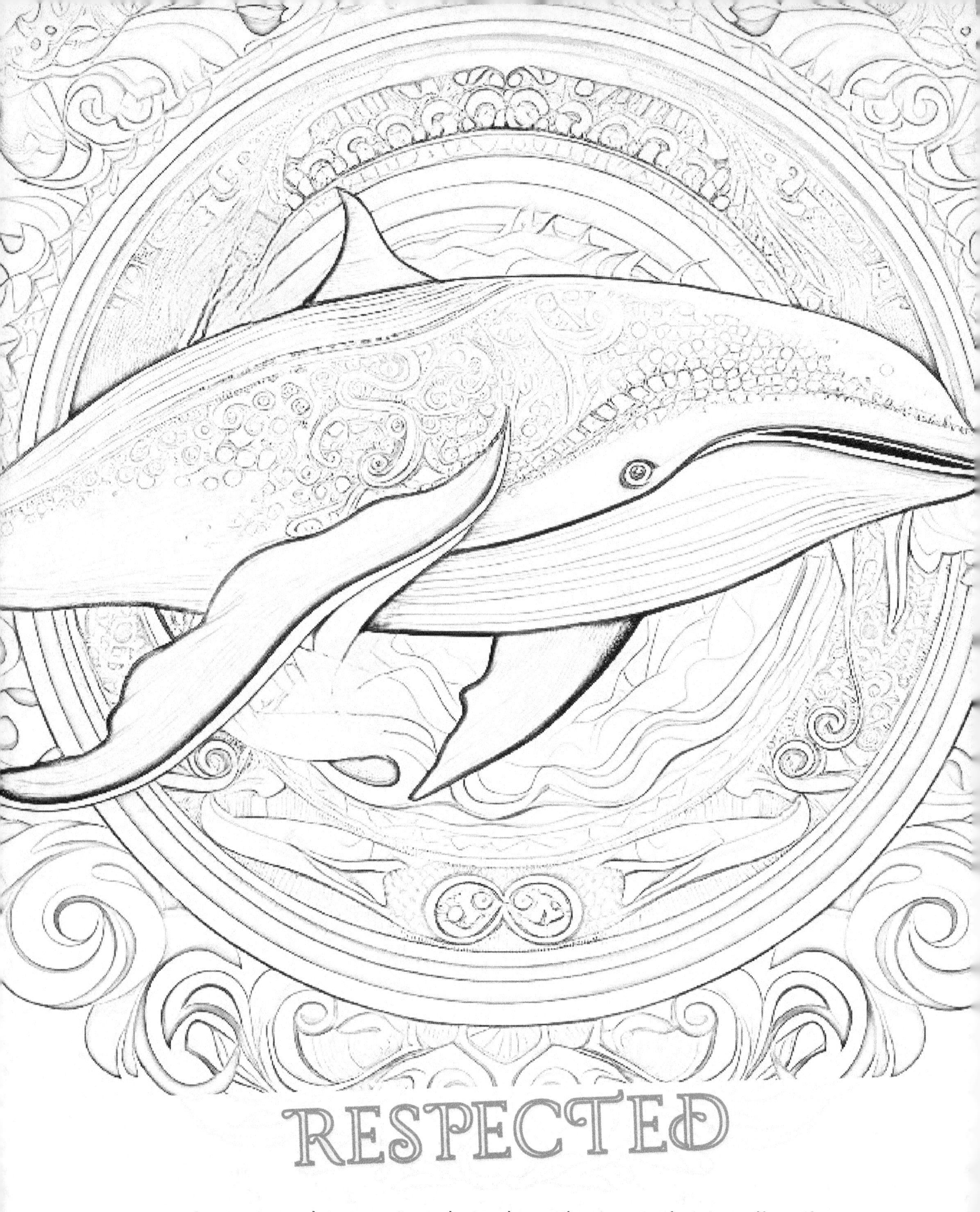

RESPECTED

I command respect and exude majesty, understanding the importance of living in balance with nature.

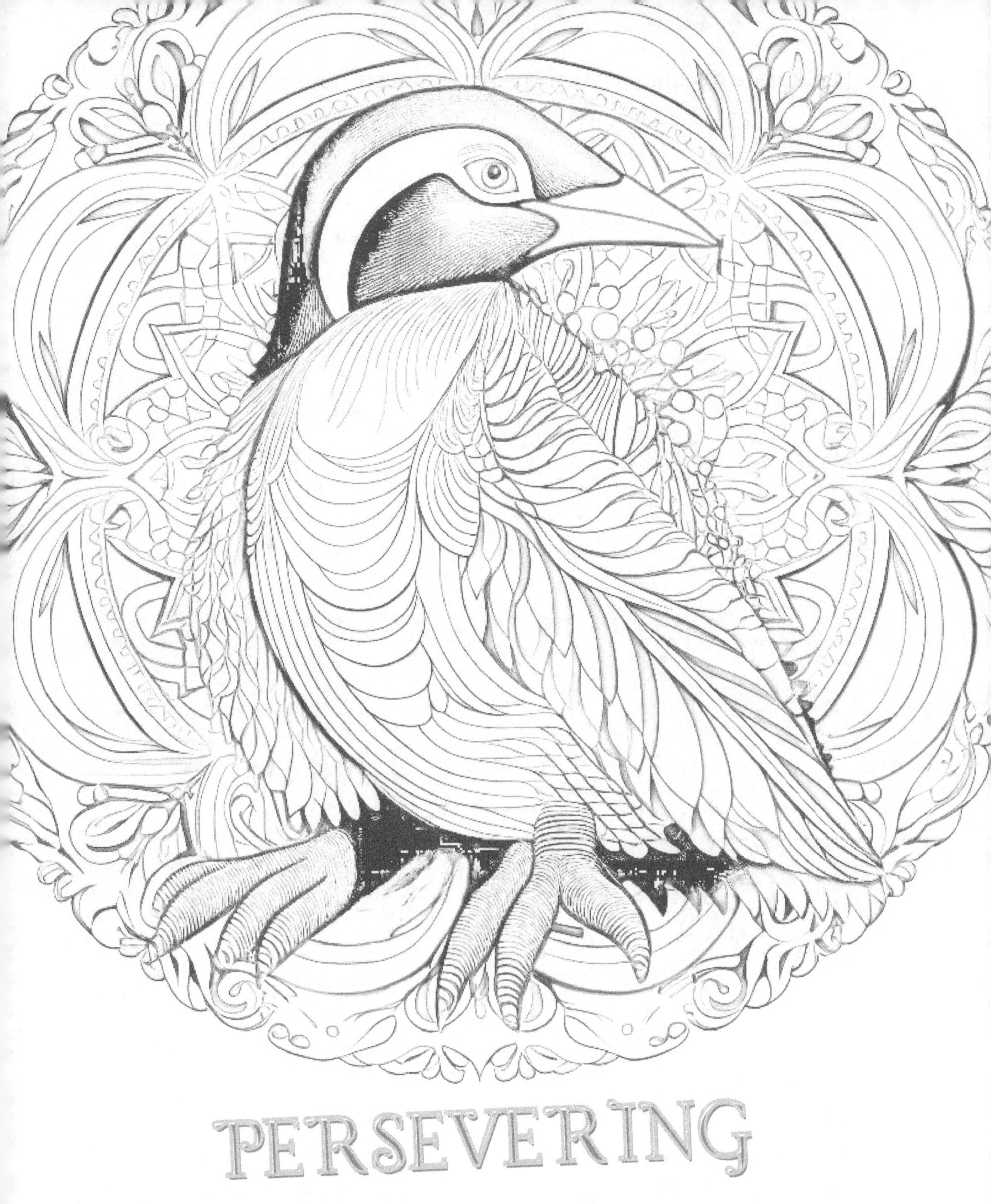

PERSEVERING

I persevere through adversity, standing tall, braving the storm, and never losing my sense of fun.

I celebrate my uniqueness. My individual stripes set me apart, and I wear them with pride.

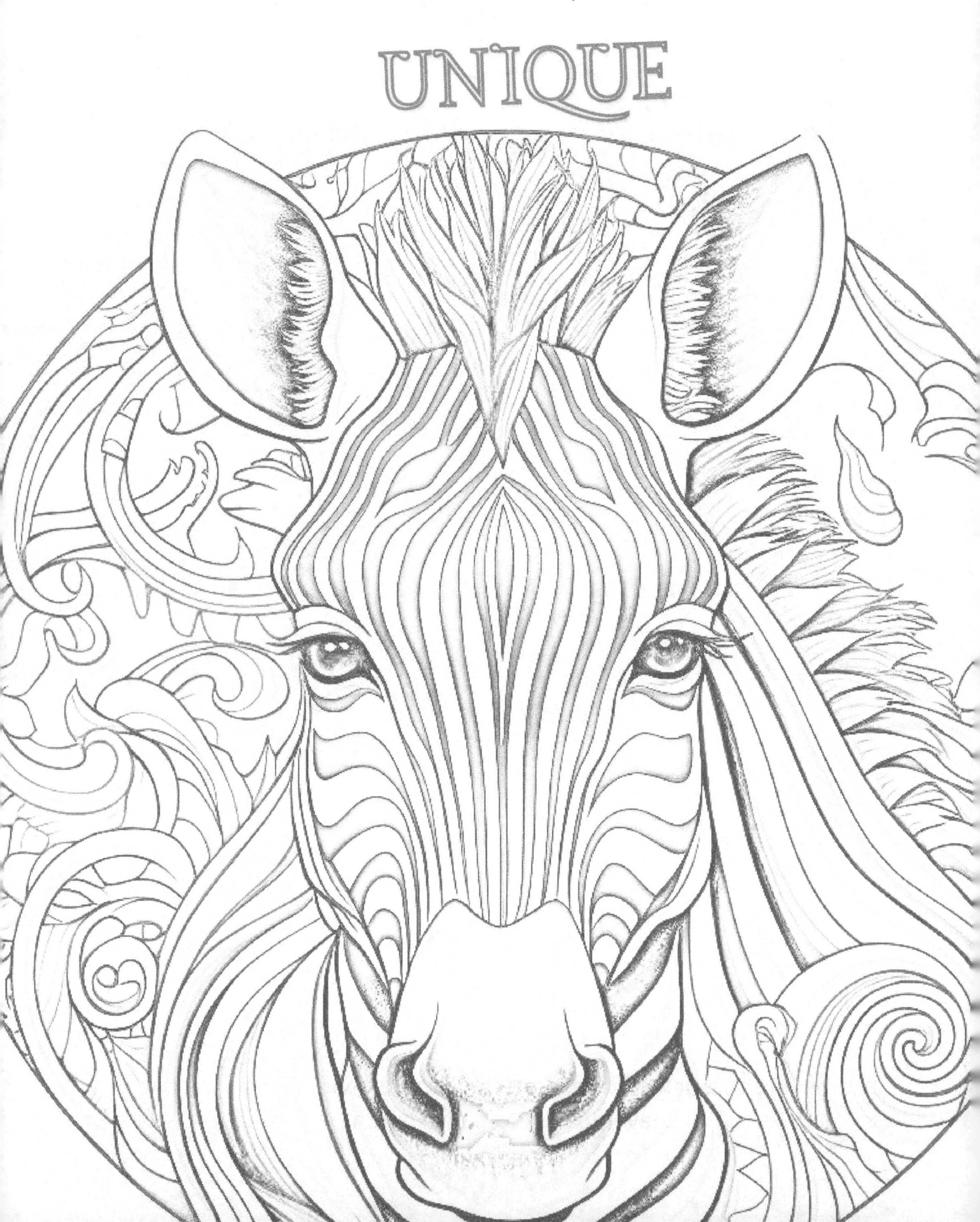

Thanks for choosing to

COLOR & EXPLORE

with us!

If you liked this coloring book, make sure to check out our other creative + educational products:

Magical Unicorns

SPACE ADVENTURE

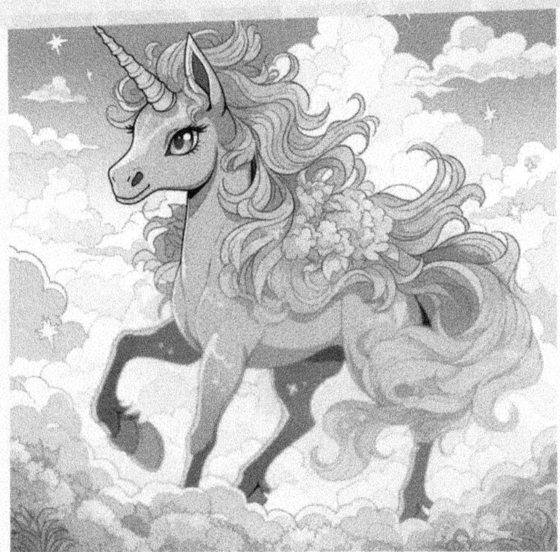

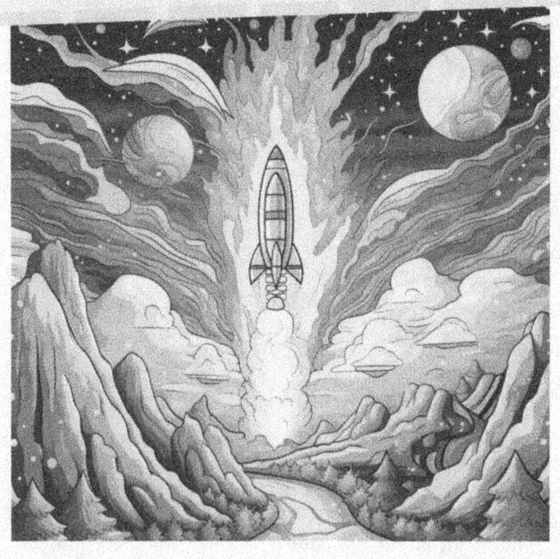

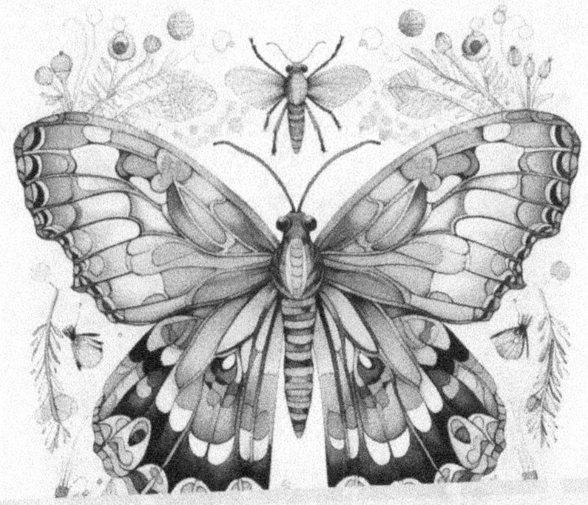

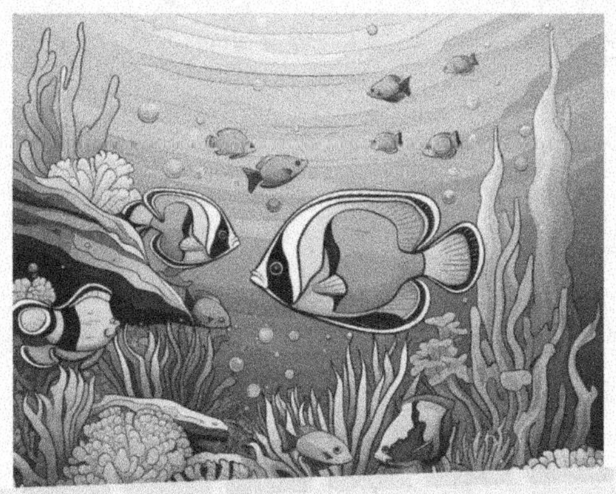

BEAUTIFUL BUGS

Ocean Deep-Dive

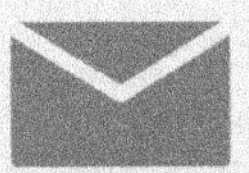

equita.publishing@gmail.com

@equita_books

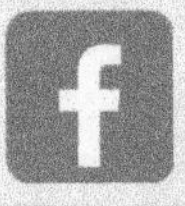

Equità Publishing

equita.publishing

EQUITÀ PUBLISHING

www.ingramcontent.com/pod-product-compliance
Lightning Source LLC
LaVergne TN
LVHW061205120826
845149LV00011B/1916

* 9 7 8 1 9 6 2 1 5 9 0 4 3 *